MARXISM AND DEMOCRACY

Marxism and Democracy

JOSEPH V. FEMIA

CLARENDON PRESS · OXFORD
1993

Oxford University Press, Walton Street, Oxford OX2 6DP

Oxford New York Toronto
Delhi Bombay Calcutta Madras Karachi
Kuala Lumpur Singapore Hong Kong Tokyo
Nairobi Dar es Salaam Cape Town
Melbourne Auckland Madrid
and associated companies in
Berlin Ibadan

Oxford is a trade mark of Oxford University Press

Published in the United States
by Oxford University Press Inc., New York

British Library Cataloguing in Publication Data
Data available

Library of Congress Cataloging in Publication Data
Femia, Joseph V.
Marxism and democracy/Joseph V. Femia.
Includes bibliographical references.
1. Communist state. 2. People's democracies. 3. Democracy.
I. Title. II. Series.
JC474.F46 1993 321.9'2—dc20 93-9236
ISBN 0–19–827494–7
ISBN 0–19–827921–3 (pbk. USA only)

Typeset by Best-set Typesetter Ltd., Hong Kong
Printed in Great Britain
on acid-free paper by
Bookcraft (Bath) Ltd
Midsomer Norton, Avon

Preface

This book arose out of a desire to challenge entrenched attitudes. For many people, Marxism is purely and simply the enemy of democracy, as illustrated by communist tyrannies the world over. For others, however, Marxism represents the highest achievement of democratic thought, whose grand ambitions were betrayed by those very same tyrannies, and only a malevolent Cold Warrior would argue otherwise. The aim of the present study is to show why the truth is much more complex than either side would allow.

An earlier version of my final, and most controversial, chapter was discussed at two workshops, convened at Glasgow and Edinburgh Universities (in September 1990 and May 1992 respectively). I am grateful to all the participants for their often critical but usually constructive comments. Two of these participants, Richard Bellamy and John Hoffman, should be singled out, as their lengthy discussions with me went well beyond the call of duty. David Miller also read the chapter in question and provided detailed observations which enabled me to strengthen it considerably. I owe him a debt of gratitude. My thanks are also due to the British Academy, which awarded me a Visiting Professorship at the European University Institute in Florence. While there, in the autumn of 1989, I benefited from discussions with numerous people, especially Steven Lukes, who merits special thanks for reading the entire manuscript, and for offering valuable advice and encouragement over a number of years. I hasten to add that none of the friends and colleagues mentioned above would necessarily endorse all my arguments.

In writing this book, I have drawn upon two of my published articles: 'Marxism and Radical Democracy', *Inquiry*, 28 (1985), 293–319; and 'Ideological Obstacles to the Political Evolution of Communist Systems', *Studies in Soviet*

Thought, 34 (1987), 215–32. Acknowledgements are due to the appropriate publishers and editors.

J.V.F.

October 1992

Contents

1 Introduction

A BOOK called *Marxism and Democracy* may elicit surprise or even derision in some quarters. Aren't the two terms in the title mutually contradictory? Is 'Marxist democracy' not an oxymoron? Yet one more bizarre product of Marxism's search for a dialectical 'unity of opposites'? In the public consciousness, Marxism is irredeemably associated with oppressive conformity and the iron rule of *nomenklatura*. As for the noble communist ideal, where men and women pursue their varied forms of self-realization in equal and total freedom, it remains a Platonic essence waiting to happen. Instead of advancing freedom, so-called Marxist regimes have perfected the instruments of repression. To Dostoevsky's famous question, 'Is everything permitted?', they answered with a resounding 'Yes', on the assumption that one could not make delicious (communist) omelettes without breaking eggs (heads). It was the wrong answer. The workers of the world have plainly united—but in opposition to the doctrine that was meant to guide them to the earthly paradise. As a blueprint for social change, Marxism is totally discredited. The disintegration of the Soviet empire only marks officially something that most people, East and West, have known for a long time. Marxism, or something that goes under that name, is still kept alive by the faithful, but only by artificial respiration.

Why, then, should we study Marxist views on democracy? There are obvious historical reasons. Whatever its (evidently lethal) failings, the doctrine inaugurated and inspired by Karl Marx has been enormously influential. Until quite recently, it reigned, in its Leninist variant, over the lives of nearly half the world's population. At one time it was regarded as the wave of the future, by friend and foe alike. When the Russians, in the 1950s, menacingly boasted to the West that 'We will bury you', no one laughed. Practical success, moreover, was matched by intellectual vigour, as Marxist methods of analysis were adopted by scholars in a wide range of disciplines, from economics to anthropology. Indeed, it is chiefly amongst intellectuals that Marxism survives today, and it is they who remind us that it once possessed, but somehow mislaid, a most admirable concern for popular self-determination. Marx and his followers attacked not only the exploitation of the workers but their powerlessness as well. Although Marxists have never been united on the precise form of democracy that would suit the communist future, they have always insisted that corrupt 'bourgeois' democracy must yield to genuine 'proletarian' democracy. In their criticisms as much as in their proposals, they contributed significantly to democratic theory, advancing a number of ideas that are by no means dead and buried. The defects of Marxist *practice* should not be allowed to obscure the occasional insights of Marxist *thought*, from which we might still benefit. Nevertheless, the practical failure of Marxism must, in the final reckoning, result from intellectual shortcomings, either in its diagnosis of society's ills or in its prescriptions for the future—or both.

One of the main purposes of this book is to explain the grotesque disparity between Marxism's emancipatory ambitions and the systematic repression carried out in its name. The question is not solely of historical interest. Even if Marxism itself is finished as a distinctive political creed, the instincts and desires it expresses will always be part of the human condition. Marxism simply represents the latest attempt to demonstrate that the pattern of the world is a logical one. Indeed, by their efforts to fit reality into an ordered and comprehensive whole, Marxists pay a kind of tribute to the grand structures of medieval theology. Marx himself denounced Christian philosophy, but rather too much, after the manner of those who are but half emancipated from the 'superstitions' they scorn. While renouncing the authority of Church and Bible, he exhibited, like the *philosophes* before him, a naïve, quasi-religious faith in the authority of Nature and Reason. What is more, the sceptic who dismantled heaven and denied that miracles ever took place nevertheless believed in the perfectibility of the human race. Marx's writings had such resonance because they reawakened the didactic/

humanitarian/religious impulse to set things right, to free mankind from ignorance, barbarism, evil, and oppression. As long as human misery stalks the planet, schemes holding out the promise of salvation—here or in the afterlife—are unlikely to fall on deaf ears.

But it is one of the great paradoxes of history that these universal remedies for the suffering of humanity, so far from curing the patient, often make the disease worse. In the case of Marxism, this paradox has been the object of extensive investigation. In what follows, I intend to show that much of this analysis is misguided, while none of it really gets to the heart of the matter. My argument will be that Marxism's 'holistic' ontology, which collapses the distance between the individual self and the 'ensemble of social relations' (Marx's words), prevents Marxists from seeing the human subject as a sovereign agent of choice, a creature who acquires his or her aims and purposes by acts of will rather than acts of discovery. Having rejected man's sovereign agency as a mystifying relic of bourgeois individualism, Marxists (or at least those working within the main Marxist tradition) have no philosophical reason for regarding the human person as the bearer of a dignity beyond the roles he inhabits or the ends he may pursue. Herein lie the seeds of Marxist totalitarianism. Of course, seeds will germinate only when soil and other environmental conditions are appropriate. Likewise, Marxist despotism cannot properly be understood in isolation from the historical circumstances and cultural limitations of those countries where it arose. In different conditions, Marxism's repressive tendencies might not have flowered. Still—and this is a point missed by those who would dissociate Marx from supposedly Marxist regimes—any explanation of what *did* happen would be incomplete if it ignored the internal logic of the theory to which all communist despots pledged their devotion.

Some may choose to see my argument as an endorsement of liberal individualism, along with all the evils it brings: greed, selfishness, exploitation, inequality. This would be a mistaken interpretation; for my purpose is simply to demonstrate a conceptual link between freedom and democracy, on the one hand, and the ontological priority of the individual self, on the other. It is not my intention to pronounce on the factual accuracy (or otherwise) of depicting human beings as sovereign choosers, as 'rival centres of the world'. Individualism in this sense is ultimately a metaphysical assumption, beyond empirical analysis. Nor do I wish to deny that this characteristically liberal assumption may itself be the root cause of many social ills. It is after all a commonplace of political theory that freedom may come into conflict with other values: say, equality, or communal solidarity, or spiritual well-being, or a sense of belonging. Liberal individualism would not seem to offer very sound philosophical underpinnings for *these* values. But, as Isaiah Berlin has pointed out time and time again, the desirable ends that men pursue are not necessarily compatible: 'Some among the Great Goods cannot live together. That is a conceptual truth. We are doomed to choose, and every choice may entail an irreparable loss.'[1] Choice, needless to say, is most effective when it is informed by a clear analysis of the available alternatives, and the present study hopes to make some small contribution in this respect.

My argument is bound to upset those Marxists who put their hero on a pedestal, asserting that this prophet of human liberation could not possibly have any connection with the authoritarian regimes that falsely claim to embody his ideas. If there must be a culprit, it is Stalin, who, we are told, departed from the authentic teachings of Marx. This ploy of (in Norberto Bobbio's apt phrase) *reductio ad Stalinum*,[2] with its assumption of Marx's innocence, is the mirror image of the opinion—favoured by the right—that Marx was Evil incarnate, a man inspired by the Devil to lead good men to their doom. Both views reduce complex issues to Manichaean dichotomies: Marx is either wicked or pure, guilty or innocent. Both views fail to appreciate how refractory reality can defeat noble intentions, how paths to Hell are often paved with such intentions. If it is absurd to blame Marx for every

---

[1] 'The Pursuit of the Ideal', in I. Berlin, *The Crooked Timber of Humanity: Chapters in the History of Ideas*, ed. H. Hardy (London: John Murray, 1990), 13.

[2] *Which Socialism?*, trans. R. Griffin and ed. R. Bellamy (Cambridge: Polity Press, 1988), 170.

'Marxist' atrocity, it is equally absurd, as we shall see in due course, to classify his works as a species of *status naturae incorruptae*.

It is now necessary to deal with a preliminary question: how do I define my basic terms, 'Marxism' and 'democracy'? At this point, the latter need not detain us for long. 'Democracy' is of course an elastic, much abused term, used as a label for regimes that are, to all appearances, directly opposed to one another in their values and practices. But one aim of this book is precisely to examine the various, even contradictory ways in which the term is deployed in Marxist discourse. I do not, at the outset, adopt one particular conception of democracy and declare all others to be false or unworthy of consideration. Indeed, I once suggested that 'it might be useful to regard democracy as an "essentially contested concept", that is, a concept whose definition and range of application is *inevitably* a matter of dispute'.[3] While I continue to stand by this statement, I propose, in the course of my argument, to explain why there must be *some* limits to how the word is used; and on this basis I shall reject the 'vanguard' model of democracy (associated with Lenin and the former Soviet regime) as a misnomer. Whether or not the reader agrees with my conceptual analysis, he or she should find that what I mean by democracy, in any particular passage, is clear from the context.

As for 'Marxism', it is a theme with many variations. Notwithstanding their fondness for intellectual systematism, Marxists find it remarkably hard to agree on the constituent components of the system in question. How, for example, can one make generalizations about a world-view whose professed adherents include both 'Eurocommunists' (who surprised the world in the 1970s by keenly defending parliamentary democracy) and Leninists (who denounce parliamentary democracy as a massive fraud, acceptable to knaves and fools only)? One could easily despair of finding order in the Tower of Babel that is Marxian thought, and yet it has but a single intellectual source—Marx himself. For all its variations,

---

[3] J. V. Femia, 'Elites, Participation and the Democratic Creed', *Political Studies*, 27 (Mar. 1979), 5.

Marxism remains a bibliocentric creed, and those who wish to explore it would be well advised to take the works of its founder as their point of departure. This does not dispose of the problem, however; for Marx was a prolific theorist, whose writings are scarcely models of clarity or consistency. It must be borne in mind that his ideas are scattered over numerous critiques and analyses, stretching over twenty-five years. There is no rounded or complete view of the whole—nothing like Plato's *Republic* or Hobbes's *Leviathan*—to eliminate the ambiguities or tie up the loose ends. No wonder Marx's disciples have always been divided into warring factions, each claiming to propound the 'real' principles of the Master, while dismissing its adversaries as heretics or worse. Simultaneously bewildered and flattered by this phenomenon, Marx is reported to have said, of some French Marxists of the 1870s, 'All I know is that I am not a Marxist.'[4] But if some of his followers misunderstood his message, he had no one to blame but himself. It is a common observation that his *œuvre* contains two possibly contradictory motifs: one scientific (social and historical change is a process dominated by inexorable laws and technological imperatives); the other, messianic or moralistic (the desire to bring forth a 'new socialist man'—free, creative, community-minded). Given this internal tension, the selective commentator may find textual evidence to vindicate a wide range of conflicting views. Those who concentrate on Marx's later writings, such as *Capital*, will interpret the doctrine as a body of scientific theorizing, from which confirmable hypotheses may be distilled. This has always been the orthodox view, enforced by the Kremlin—Marxism's functional analogue to the Vatican. Other observers, focusing on the earlier works, understand Marxism as essentially a moral doctrine of freedom, concerned to emancipate men and women from the shadowy constructions of their own minds. Stress is laid on reflective human agency, not on iron laws similar to those of physics. Each of these interpretations, moreover, allows for a variety of permutations. The possibilities seem endless.

A further source of confusion has been the tendency,

---

[4] Quoted by Engels in a letter to C. Schmidt, 5 Aug. 1890.

especially pronounced since the end of the Second World War, to combine Marx's philosophy with other apparently anti-thetical philosophies. In recent years, for example, fertile and imaginative thinkers, bored by stale orthodoxy, have tried to reinvigorate Marxism by forcing it into 'strange shotgun marriages'[5] with psychoanalysis (Erich Fromm, Herbert Marcuse), existentialism (Jean-Paul Sartre), structuralism (Louis Althusser), and phenomenology (Enzo Paci). The motivation to produce such curious hybrids was powerful. For it was not always possible to press what William James called the 'irreducible brute facts' into the neat categories prescribed by Marxist faith. It was therefore necessary to seek, beneath the literal significance of the authoritative texts, hidden meanings—meanings often inconsistent with the ones normally found. One manifestation of this 'creative' approach has been to 'vindicate' Marxism by divesting it of its most controversial and distinctive ideas. The new type of Marxist apologist attacks not the criticisms but the critics, who are invariably accused of misunderstanding Marx and setting up a straw man. Such apologists are often quite convincing in their endeavours to prove that Marx did not actually mean what nearly everyone else thought he meant. But with saviours like this Marxism has no need of enemies. After all the subtle reinterpretation is complete, what is left to distinguish Marxism as a creed? One is reminded of the American commander during the Vietnam war who announced that it was necessary to destroy the town of Hue in order to 'save' it. As long ago as 1918, Antonio Gramsci—himself a heterodox interpreter of Marx—compared the adjective 'Marxist' to 'money that has been worn out from passing through too many hands'.[6] By now, it could be argued, the money has lost its face value and should be withdrawn from circulation: Marxism, that is to say, no longer means anything in particular. If this were so, it would be difficult to conduct a coherent analysis of Marxism's relationship to democracy—or to anything else for that matter. We could not talk about Marxism at all.

[5] N. Bobbio, *Which Socialism?*, 169.
[6] 'Il Nostro Marx', *Il Grido del Popolo*, 4 May 1918; reprinted in A. Gramsci, *Scritti giovanili: 1914–1918* (Turin: Einaudi, 1958), 220.

It should be noted, however, that Marx himself disapproved of indiscriminate political labelling. He was keen to distinguish his own ideas from those of other socialist thinkers—reformist, Utopian, anarchist, Blanquist—and this determination to preserve a distinctive place for Marxism within the wider socialist tradition is still valid. Despite its variety, Marxism is not an open-ended doctrine. Steven Lukes has written that 'the marxist tradition is no monolithic unity, but a contested terrain'.[7] True enough. Let us pursue the metaphor, however. While contested terrain does not necessarily have fixed boundaries, it must possess certain topographical features that enable us to distinguish it from other pieces of land. Similarly, we can isolate a cluster of characteristics that are undoubtedly present, and prominent, in the canonical Marxist texts. There are at least six such characteristics, all of which will receive further discussion in subsequent chapters:

(i) *Holism*. The assumption that the social whole takes priority, both methodologically and morally, over its individual human components;

(ii) *The primacy of economics*. The belief that human thought and institutions must ultimately be explained by the methods and techniques we adopt to transform nature in pursuit of our material needs;

(iii) *Class analysis*. The view of society as a structure of hierarchically arranged, and inherently antagonistic, classes, differentiated on the basis of position and function in the organization of production;

(iv) *Commitment to revolution*. The transition from capitalism to socialism requires a qualitative, though not necessarily violent, change; a once-and-for-all upheaval;

(v) *Historical determinism*. The idea that socialism is the logical consequence of capitalism's internal dynamics and not merely a desirable goal or ideal;

(vi) *Communism*. The conviction that the final goal of history is a classless, stateless society, marked by social ownership of the means of production, equality of reward as

---

[7] *Marxism and Morality* (Oxford: Clarendon Press, 1985), 2.

well as opportunity, and pervasive communal solidarity and harmony.

Without claiming that each characteristic is definitive, and that those who reject it are thereby excommunicate from the Marxist Church, I *would* contend that anyone who declines to identify with the bulk of these basic ideas can with little justification declare himself a Marxist, unless the term is to be drained of all meaning. However diverse its particular forms may be, Marxism exhibits a 'central structure of thinking'[8] that enables us to speak intelligibly about the doctrine's strengths and shortcomings, its potentialities and limitations. And, to repeat, this 'central structure' is primarily derived from the writings of Marx himself.

It should go without saying, however, that each of the constituent features listed above is itself open to interpretation. In elucidating Marx's thought, I shall be compelled, at various points, to opt for one interpretation rather than another. Where such selection is necessary, I shall either adopt the standard reading (the one favoured by the scholarly consensus) or else provide arguments and evidence for an alternative. I realize that it will be impossible to please all of the Marx scholars all of the time. Let me beg their indulgence. Given that I must cover the whole of the Marxist tradition, space does not permit me to intervene in every exegetical controversy. In any case, the subject of this book is Marxism, not Marx. For my purposes, the way in which his ideas were understood by his most influential followers is, in a sense, more important than 'what Marx *really* said', as divined by highly specialized scholars, employing the refined philological techniques of the medieval Schoolmen. Such scholarship has its uses (and who would quarrel with the quest for historical accuracy?), but it is no more valid to reduce Marxism to the intentions of Marx than to identify Christianity with the intentions of Christ, not least because the intentions of great prophets (even divinely inspired ones!) are often obscure or contradictory, and therefore require interpretation by their disciples.

How, then, will my analysis proceed? I shall begin by

[8] Ibid.

examining the various Marxist criticisms of liberal democracy. These, as will be seen, arise from two of Marxism's most dubious dogmas: holism and economic reductionism. Chapter 3 will discuss what, if anything, Marxists would put in place of the parliamentary state. It will be shown that there is considerable confusion and disarray amongst Marxists on this crucial matter. The root of the problem, I shall argue, is that there is no recognizable form of democracy that can accommodate all of Marxism's contradictory goals: active popular participation *and* all-embracing central planning; human liberation *and* submission to the dialectical truths embedded in the historical process. My concluding chapter will try to explain why Marxism's internal contradictions have always, in practice, been 'solved' through despotic imposition. Leninists attempted to deal with this uncomfortable reality by redefining democracy, such that, in its 'higher' or 'proletarian' guise, it actually equates with despotism. However, this Orwellian stratagem only served to highlight the chasm between participatory ideal and oligarchic practice. Why is it that Marxism's repressive tendencies invariably overwhelm its emancipatory aims? As previously stated, my argument will point to Marxism's tragic flaw: its rejection of the ontological, and hence moral, ultimacy of the individual. This holistic premise, when taken to its logical conclusion, is largely responsible for transforming the Marxist project of liberation into its exact opposite.

In mounting my case, I shall focus on themes, not individuals. In consequence, some readers may find that their favourite Marxist is either ignored or mentioned only *en passant*. It is essential to remember that this book is not a survey of what every interesting Marxist (or post-Marxist) thinker had to say about democracy. Limitations of space force me to be selective when it comes to individual writers, though I would claim that my coverage of the main Marxist ideas on the subject is comprehensive.

2 The Marxist Critique of Liberal Democracy

I Theoretical Foundations

THE MARXIAN indictment of liberal democracy rests upon what Engels referred to as 'historical materialism'—the cornerstone of all Marxist analysis. It therefore seems appropriate, as a preliminary step, to sketch out the essentials of this philosophy of human evolution. Marx developed his system in opposition to idealism, a characteristically German mode of thinking which portrayed the world as if it were dancing to the tune of abstract ideas. For Hegel, the doyen of this school, history was the progressive unfolding of 'Spirit' (*Geist*), striving to realize its essence. Marx dismissed such speculation as mystical nonsense, no less impenetrable than the enigmas of Christian theology. Empirical observation alone could deliver the truths of existence: 'Let us rebel against the rule of thoughts', he declared.[1] This rebellion received its lengthiest expression in an early work (1846) called *The German Ideology*, where Marx argued that man's productive interchange with nature was the real subtext of history. Human beings, he maintained, are defined not by ideal essences, 'the phantoms of their imagination',[2] but by the totality of actions whereby they reproduce their own material existence: 'What they are, therefore, coincides ... with *what* they produce and *how* they produce.'[3] A number of conclusions follow. To begin with, political and legal systems reflect underlying economic pressures rather than their own autonomous principles: 'The social structure

---

[1] *The German Ideology*, in *Writings of the Young Marx on Philosophy and Society*, trans. and ed. L. D. Easton and K. H. Guddat (New York: Doubleday, 1967), 404.
[2] Ibid.
[3] Ibid. 409.

and the state continually evolve out of the life-process of definite individuals, ... as they work, produce materially, and act under definite material limitations, presuppositions, and conditions.' The mental life of society is similarly derivative: 'Conceiving, thinking, and the intellectual relationships of men appear here as the direct result of their material behaviour.' Religion, morality, philosophy—these are not embodiments of eternal truth but 'necessary sublimations of man's material life-process'. Whereas the idealists saw the real world as an expression of metaphysical substance, of 'the phantoms formed in the human brain', the contrary is true: 'In direct contrast to German philosophy, which descends from heaven to earth, here one ascends from earth to heaven.'[4]

Thirteen years later, in his famous Preface to his *Critique of Political Economy*, Marx made the most concise and systematic statement of his theory:

In the social production which men carry on they enter into definite relations that are indispensable and independent of their will; these relations of production correspond to a definite stage of development of their material powers of production. The sum total of these relations of production constitutes the economic structure of society— the real foundation, on which rise legal and political superstructures and to which correspond definite forms of social consciousness. The mode of production in material life determines the general character of the social, political and spiritual processes of life. It is not the consciousness of men that determines their existence, but, on the contrary, their social existence determines their consciousness.

Marx here posits a functional relationship between 'material powers of production' (i.e. tools, machines, skills, raw materials, technical processes) and all other aspects of life. Ideas and social institutions develop and prosper if, and only if, they suit the productive system. But in Marx's dialectical scheme nothing is permanent: what was once progressive eventually becomes regressive and must be superseded.

At a certain stage of their development the material forces of production in society come into conflict with the existing relations of

---

[4] Ibid. 413–15.

production, or—what is but a legal expression for the same thing—with the property relations within which they had been at work before. From forms of development of the forces of production these relations turn into their fetters. Then comes the period of social revolution. With the change of the economic foundation the entire immense superstructure is more or less rapidly transformed.

This model of historical change perfectly exemplifies the priorities of the theory: not lofty ideals but hard economic realities spawn great revolutionary upheavals. Next, the Preface asserts that the historical evolution of humanity is divided into phases by the different forms that production assumes:

In broad outline we can designate the Asiatic, the ancient, the feudal, and the modern bourgeois methods of production as so many epochs in the progress of the economic formation of society. The bourgeois relations of production are the last antagonistic form of the social process of production—antagonistic not in the sense of individual antagonism, but of one arising from conditions surrounding the life of individuals in society; at the same time the productive forces developing in the womb of bourgeois society create the material conditions for the solution of that antagonism. This social formation constitutes, therefore, the closing chapter of the prehistoric stage of human society.[5]

For Marx an 'antagonistic' society is one divided into classes (though, for some reason, neither the word 'class' nor its plural appears in the Preface). Social divisions arise, historically, when surplus production is generated, such that it becomes possible for a class of non-producers to live off the productive activity of others. Those who gain control of the means of production form a 'ruling class', established through a combination of state repression and ideological camouflage. Class relations, says Marx, are necessarily exploitative and imply fundamental divisions of interest between ruling and subordinate classes. These relations are also inherently conflictual, giving rise to overt struggle in those periods when the relations of production (the system of property ownership) come into contradiction with, or become 'fetters' on, the

[5] In *Marx & Engels: Basic Writings on Politics and Philosophy*, ed. L. S. Feuer (New York: Doubleday, 1959), 43–4.

productive forces. Such struggles form the chief mechanism or 'motor' of historical development. Modern bourgeois society is marked by one dominant exploitative relationship—that between those who own capital (capitalists) and those who own only their labour power (wage workers, or proletarians). This relationship has become an impediment to economic growth and efficiency, primarily because the need to sell goods at a profit increasingly conflicts with the meagre purchasing power of the exploited masses. As capitalism slides inexorably towards rack and ruin, the sole and unavoidable solution is revolution and the establishment of communism: a form of social life without classes, where the means of production are owned by the community collectively. 'Prehistory' comes to an end and genuine human history begins. Why communism should be immune to the dialectical process of disintegration that afflicts every other social order is never adequately explained. It is simply assumed that the absence of *class* contradictions means the absence of *all* contradictions.

While Marx ridiculed the mystical properties of idealism, which 'descends from heaven to earth', the structure of his own theory was teleological and Hegelian: mankind is progressing, in accordance with a discernible pattern, towards some predefined goal. In his ringing declaration:

It is a question of these laws themselves, of these tendencies working with iron necessity towards inevitable results. The country that is more developed industrially only shows, to the less developed, the image of its own future.[6]

But, to the eternal bemusement of his critics, Marx saw nothing metaphysical or unscientific in this attempt to reduce the whole of history to a single scheme. Quite the reverse. To him, belief in objective historical necessity was the essential difference between his own 'scientific' socialism

[6] Author's preface to the first edition of *Capital* (1867), in *Marx & Engels: Basic Writings*, 135. In a preface to the second edition (1873, p. 143), Marx confirms that his intention is to show 'the necessity of successive determinate orders of social conditions'.

and the socialism of his 'Utopian' predecessors. His theoretical descendants agreed. Marxism, in its classical form, is thus deterministic, predictive, and generalizing. Imitating the natural sciences, it searches for causes of phenomena, and makes predictions about future events.

This outline of Marx's theory, necessarily brief and simplified, prompts difficult questions that have exercised commentators for over a century. Here we can do little more than mention them. In particular, if, as Marx says, men are governed by material powers and relations that are 'independent of their will', does this mean that the life of the mind is an epiphenomenon, embodying no active principle? Further, if, as Marx also says, the mode of production determines the 'legal and political superstructures', are we to understand these 'superstructures' as mere by-products, devoid of independence or causal efficacy? The answer to both questions is almost certainly no. As we shall see when examining Marx's views on the (so-called) capitalist state, there was often tension between his theoretical statements, on the one hand, and his actual accounts of historical events, on the other. When summarizing his basic explanatory framework, he revealed a predilection for sharp and memorable formulations; but when applying this framework to the real world, he showed some respect for the variety of human experience, which could not easily be captured by sweeping generalizations. This complication notwithstanding, we can confidently assume that historical materialism, whether interpreted loosely or stringently, gives causal primacy to economic factors, and that this theoretical commitment underpins the Marxian critique of liberal democracy, to which we now turn. Since Marx never produced a lengthy, methodical account of the modern state, his views must be pieced together from various sources: philosophical reflections, incidental remarks, and observations on contemporary history. Nevertheless, certain patterns do emerge with clarity, and later Marxists have done no more than restate or elaborate his core ideas. We shall do well, therefore, to focus on Marx himself. His critique takes two forms: philosophical and (for want of a better word) sociological.

II   Philosophical Critique

Marx's philosophical objections to liberal democracy are set out in his youthful writings, which express a broad concern with the effects of modernity—capitalism, in particular—on the fabric of social life. For our purposes, the main works to be examined are his *Critique of Hegel's Philosophy of the State*, written in 1843, and his 1845 essay 'On the Jewish Question', both of which explore a central theme—the peculiarly modern split between 'civil society', as the battle of private material interests, and 'the state', as an abstract, ideal universality. The division between these two spheres of contemporary life had previously been investigated by Hegel, who defined civil society as the totality of divergent particular interests that arise from the system of private property. The guiding principle of civil society is the individual's pursuit of his own selfish ends—in a word, egoism, which is given free rein in the capitalist exchange economy. At the same time, this self-seeking individual is a participant in political life, where he transcends egoism and behaves as a public-spirited citizen. Hegel saw no insoluble contradiction between the impartial demands of citizenship and the maximization of private utilities. He was confident that the conflicts within civil society could be rationally resolved in the supreme will of the modern state, a form of association (potentially) independent of particular interests. Here personal individuality and communal responsibility, individual rights and social duty, private man and public man are finally united in a higher synthesis. But while civil society is superseded by the state, its essential features are (or should be) preserved:

The state is actual, and its actuality consists in this, that the interest of the whole is realized in and through particular ends. Actuality is always the unity of universal and particular, the universal dismembered in the particulars which seem to be self-subsistent, although they really are upheld and contained only in the whole.[7]

Hegel understood that modern civilization, with its competitive relationships and rigorous division of labour, caused the

---

[7] *Hegel's Philosophy of Right*, trans. and ed. T. M. Knox (Oxford: Clarendon Press, 1952), 283, addition 162.

estrangement of the individual from the state and the larger community. To solve this problem it was necessary, in his view, to strike a harmonious balance between the organic basis of social life (the universal) and the individual subject's desire for autonomy (the particular). But reconciliation would come not through radical restructuring, nor through an uncritical worship of the past. Revolutionaries forget the power of traditional loyalties, while reactionaries take futile stands against the evolutionary process. Instead, we should reflect upon the virtues of the present. Spiritual union with one's fellow-citizens, the abolition of estrangement, requires an adequate theoretical grasp of how the institutions of liberal political life (independent bureaucracies, representative assemblies, constitutional monarchs) effect 'the unity of universal and particular', of communal obligation and bourgeois individualism. The remedy for alienation, that uniquely modern affliction, lies before our very eyes, 'in the great edifice of the state'.[8] It is here that the human spirit ends its historical quest for fulfilment, as 'essence' and 'reality' finally come together in a rational form of political organization.

Marx praised Hegel for recognizing human estrangement, but attacked him for resting content with a delusive solution. To Marx, Hegel's political analysis was fatally flawed by his idealist attempt to derive empirical institutions from the development of the 'Idea', history's 'essence' or 'final cause'. Thus empirical reality is 'pronounced rational, but it is not rational through its own rationality but rather because the empirical fact in its empirical existence has another meaning than its own. The initial fact is not taken as such but rather as a mystical result.'[9] From this perspective of 'pantheistic mysticism',[10] the *status quo* acquires a philosophical halo, whose luminance blinds Hegel to the ugly truth. The state in anything like its present form does not provide the arena wherein man overcomes his egoism and strives for the common good; political society is an empty ideal sphere, an illusory community, where man is 'an imaginary member of

---

[8] Ibid. 288, addition 170.
[9] *Critique of Hegel's Philosophy of the State*, in *Writings of the Young Marx*, 157.
[10] Ibid. 155.

an imagined sovereignty, divested of his actual individual life and endowed with an unactual universality'.[11] Under capitalism, Marx explains, only 'economic man', only the private person who belongs to civil society, possesses real, concrete existence; as a citizen, he is merely part of an abstraction, the political community, a fantastic projection of man's self-image as a communal being. Politics, when divorced from the daily activity of earning a living, is without content or useful purpose. From the objective standpoint of ordinary citizens, the representative state is distant and remote, unresponsive to their real concerns—the exploitation and human isolation they suffer under capitalism. Yet the fictitious equality and fellowship of their idealized political world serve to conceal the inequality and strife in the 'mundane existence of their actuality'.[12] In 'actuality', as in Hegel's philosophy itself, true reality is hidden by a process of abstraction. What is more, the dichotomy between state and economic life conveys the impression that relations within the latter are not susceptible to the collective control and discussion that, in principle at least, characterize the former. Principles, however, should not be confused with reality. The modern state, even in its most democratic guise, is in no way a neutral arbiter standing above social divisions. Instead of transcending the disunity of civil society, it perpetuates this condition, by reinforcing the competitiveness of private existence together with the domination of property. Indeed, the so-called representatives of the people are nothing but spokesmen for powerful economic groups who finance their campaigns and pay them bribes. As for the civil service, Hegel's 'universal class' supposedly devoted to the general interest, they transform the state's purpose into their own 'private purpose of *hunting for higher positions* and *making a career*'.[13]

For Marx, then, the state ('imagined sovereignty') is to civil society ('the real nature of things') as heaven is to earth.[14] The heaven of the bourgeois liberal state, like the Christian's

---

[11] 'On the Jewish Question', in *Writings of the Young Marx*, 226.
[12] *Critique of Hegel's Philosophy of the State*, in *Writings of the Young Marx*, 176, 199–202.
[13] Ibid. 186.
[14] 'On the Jewish Question', in *Writings of the Young Marx*, 226.

heaven, expresses an imaginary, 'unreal' universality. Political abstractions, in common with religious ones, arise as compensation for the non-realization of man's ideal aims within his profane or material existence—man's real existence, according to the canons of historical materialism. Oppressed creatures cling to illusions in order to assuage their anxiety and despair. The only way to abolish these illusions is to abolish the conditions that produce them. One wonders how Marx expected the masses to break out of this vicious circle. For on his account, both the capitalist system and the liberal state reduce them to dumb passivity. Rather than active participants, full of confidence, they become mindless spectators, ripe for manipulation. Social pathology is reflected in individual psychology.

Corresponding to the social division between 'private' and 'public' is a dualism within each person, who regards himself as both a private individual (*homme*) seeking his own advantage, and an altruistic citizen (*citoyen*) pursuing the common good. This split was first highlighted a century earlier by Jean-Jacques Rousseau, who saw bourgeois man as at odds with himself, forever veering between private inclination and civic duty. Hegel, too, acknowledged the bifurcation of the human personality into separate spheres of privacy, on the one hand, and universality, on the other. Like Herder and Schiller before him, he was disturbed by the disintegration of the 'whole man', the man of ancient Greece, who shared in the total experience available in society and drew no distinction between his personal and public duties. But, echoing his German predecessors, Hegel deemed psychological dualism an inevitable consequence of mankind's spiritual development, a process demanding specialization and differentiation. The clock could not be turned back. Fundamental changes in the human condition precluded any attempt to revive the natural, unreflective solidarity of the ancients. Personal independence and individual conscience were essential to modern notions of selfhood. Nevertheless, Hegel believed that the two disparate elements within the individual psyche (the self-centred and the communal), like the two disparate elements within society (the economic and the political), could be synthesized by the modern representative state, in whose activities men find 'their substantive self-conciousness' and realize 'the universal implicit in their particular interests'.[15] In other words, we overcome the fragmentation of our being, and find inner peace, when we understand that the contradiction between private and social life is more apparent than real, that the one presupposes the other.

For Marx, no such tranquillity is possible as long as capitalism persists. Yet again, in his estimation, Hegel's conclusions amount to an uncritical acceptance of bourgeois ills in the guise of their resolution. Yet again, verbal legerdemain becomes a substitute for practical remedies. For until capitalism is banished from this earth, man will continue to suffer inner turmoil, to see himself as shopkeeper *and* citizen, labourer *and* citizen, landlord *and* citizen. But, since citizenship has no basis in his 'mundane existence', it is experienced as an alien or false identity, to be assumed at odd intervals for ritual puposes. According to Marx, this frustration of our healthy, gregarious instincts induces a feeling of existential loneliness, as calculating individuals eye each other suspiciously in the capitalist market-place.

On this analysis, the bourgeois state mocks man. Rather than enabling him to associate in community with other men as a 'species-being', it expresses 'the *separation* of man from his *community*, from himself and from other men'.[16] Liberal democracy, in sum, manifests alienation in three senses: (i) it severs man from his society by making him 'an imaginary member of an imagined sovereignty', who views political life as 'remote from his actual individuality';[17] (ii) it both mirrors and sanctions the struggle of man against man in civil society, the sphere of '*bellum omnium contra omnes*';[18] and (iii) it fosters a split within the human personality between private interest and communal obligation or allegiance—a disharmony which, under capitalism, is inevitably resolved in favour of egoism. In bourgeois society, then, human beings are alienated from their essential social nature and grotesquely transformed, by the values and institutions of that society,

---

[15] *Hegel's Philosophy of Right*, 163.
[16] 'On the Jewish Question', in *Writings of the Young Marx*, 226–7.
[17] Ibid. 226, 231.
[18] Ibid. 227.

into isolated 'monads', torn apart by conflicting pressures and estranged from their very humanity as well as other men. Marx, in his polemic against liberal aims and practices, continues Aristotle's old line: man is, by nature, a *zōon politikon*, who finds fulfilment in public activity and never sees his different roles in life as mutually exclusive or inconsistent with one another. Marx's ideal is the 'whole man' of ancient Greece. In capitalist democracy, by contrast, man is 'lost and alienated', 'not yet an *actual* species-being'.[19]

Marx makes it clear that the types of alienation discussed above are uniquely modern scourges. In the ancient polis, blessed with an almost organic unity, egoistic indifference to the community was inconceivable and the public/private distinction had yet to emerge. In the Middle Ages, the division of society into estates, corporations, and guilds represented a departure from the unmediated 'one-ness' of classical antiquity; but these private associations had a directly political function. As Marx puts it, '. . . property, trade, society, man was *political* . . . each private sphere had a political character or was one political sphere, and politics was characteristic of the private spheres'. He continues: 'In the Middle Ages the political constitution was the constitution of private property but only because the constitution of private property was political. In the Middle Ages the life of the people and the life of the state were identical.'[20] Trade and property were 'unfree', subject to political controls, and 'public' and 'private' were closely linked through intermediary bodies (estates, corporations, guilds). A kind of spontaneous, if limited, solidarity prevailed, with human beings bound together by traditional ties of duty and loyalty.

The bourgeois revolution set out to destroy all this—to liberate people from inherited bonds. It 'thereby *abolished the political character of civil society*' and freed the political realm 'from its entanglement with civil life'. As economic activity was relieved of political constraints on the disposal of property and labour, the state acquired an abstract universality which purported to render class distinctions irrelevant.

[19] Ibid. 231.
[20] *Critique of Hegel's Philosophy of the State*, in *Writings of the Young Marx*, 176.

But, Marx observes, 'the fulfillment of the idealism of the state was at the same time the fulfillment of the materialism of civil society. The throwing off of the political yoke was at the same time the throwing off of the bond that had fettered the egoistic spirit of civil society'.[21] The process of political emancipation, which culminated in the French Revolution, dissolved civil life into its constituent elements: self-absorbed, independent individuals, released from communal obligations and left to rampage like wild beasts in the capitalist jungle.

Since, in Marx's opinion, civil society is the real basis of human life and the political state only its ethereal projection, it follows that the regime of private property, contract, and competition shapes the 'emancipated' state and finds expression in the formal freedoms proclaimed by the 'so-called *rights of man*' (as Marx contemptuously called them).[22] For him, such rights were either the product of exceptional delusion or just ordinary cant, reflecting the wish of the capitalist entrepreneur to be free from social responsibility. Marx refused to believe that people possessed categorical rights, logically prior to the collective and flowing directly from human nature. To begin with, he denied the existence of an abstract human essence—the transcendental foundation of natural rights doctrine. According to his much-quoted sixth Thesis on Feuerbach (1845), 'the essence of man is no abstraction inhering in each single individual. In its actuality it is the ensemble of social relationships.'[23] To locate the 'actuality' of the human essence in the historically fleeting 'ensemble of social relationships' is, in effect, to do away with the concept of human essence as such. But the rights of man are, by definition, moral entitlements based on fixed and abstract human qualities or capacities, not on particular social arrangements or preferences that might vary over time and space. For instance, Tom Paine, an exemplar of Enlightenment thought, deduces such rights from the universal 'truth' that 'all men are born equal' and created in God's 'own image'.[24] The sixth Thesis is not just an isolated remark; two

---

[21] 'On the Jewish Question', in *Writings of the Young Marx*, 239.
[22] Ibid. 235.
[23] 'Theses on Feuerbach', in *Writings of the Young Marx*, 402.
[24] *The Rights of Man* (Harmondsworth, Middx.: Penguin, 1969), 88–9.

years earlier in his critique of Hegel (to take but one example) Marx protested that 'man is not an abstract being squatting outside the world. Man is the *world of men*, the state, society.'[25]

While such remarks seem clear enough, some ambiguity lingers. For in manuscripts composed almost simultaneously with the works containing the above quotations, Marx explicitly endorsed the idea of a human essence, referring to man as a 'social being', or (more often) a 'species-being' (*Gattungwessen*).[26] Indeed, this concept of man, as we have already seen, underlies his theory of political alienation. At best, Marx, in these early writings, was none too precise in his use of language; at worst, he was muddled. The orthodox Marxist view, notably formulated by Louis Althusser, is that the young Marx, still under the baleful influence of German philosophy, nevertheless caught occasional glimpses of his later, scientific theory, which definitely ruled out the ascription of metaphysical essences to concrete objects. Althusser, along with many others, sees the sixth Thesis as a watershed: 'In 1845, Marx broke radically with every theory that based history and politics on an essence of man.'[27] The trouble with this interpretation is that even in Marx's mature works, including *Capital*, references (both direct and oblique) to 'human nature' and 'man' as a 'social animal' still appear, albeit with less frequency.[28] We can go some way towards solving the puzzle if we recognize that 'human nature' is an internally complex concept with, arguably, two dimensions. Firstly, there is the *descriptive* or *factual* dimension, which singles out certain human capacities, dispositions, and properties. When, say, Hobbes informs us that human beings are innately self-seeking and aggressive, he is making a descriptive statement about actual reality as he perceives it. But the

---

[25] 'Toward the Critique of Hegel's Philosophy of Law: Introduction', in *Writings of the Young Marx*, 250. See also *The German Ideology* (ibid. 409), where Marx maintains that the 'nature of individuals thus depends on the material conditions which determine their production'.

[26] 'On the Jewish Question' and *Economic and Philosophic Manuscripts* (1844), in *Writings of the Young Marx*, 226–7, 231, 241, 294–5, 306.

[27] *For Marx*, trans. B. Brewster (New York: Vintage Books, 1970), 227–8.

[28] See, for example, *Capital*, iii (Moscow: Foreign Languages Publishing House, 1959), 800; *Capital*, i (Harmondsworth, Middx.: Penguin, 1976), 443–4.

concept of human nature also has a (usually implicit) *normative* or *prescriptive* dimension. The statement 'X is man's essence' is sometimes another way of saying that 'X *ought to be* man's aim', that we become truly human only when we act in one way rather than another. From the vast range of contradictory human aspirations and values, a certain sub-set is selected and pronounced essential to human well-being. Marx's various statements about our essential social nature seem to fall into this category. Direct evidence for my interpretation can be found in the passage, in Marx's reflections on the 'Jewish question', where he implores man to '*become* a species-being', thus implying that a communal disposition is a *goal* or *potentiality* rather than an *actual characteristic* of human beings.[29] But does this moral injunction not contradict the intrinsic relativism of Marx's materialist outlook, which—please recall—reduces ideas and principles to transient economic relations? Not necessarily. Although his terminology lacks rigour, we can clarify matters, on his behalf, by relating the supposed need for communal attachment to the present requirements of the evolving production process. From the materialist perspective, the equation of communal living with the good life is not a universal truth, derived from some abstract essence, but the result of historically created possibilities and needs. So Marx's indignant response to the rampant egoism of bourgeois society is perhaps compatible with historical materialism. But the confusing fact remains that he occasionally expressed this moral indignation in the language of those he condemned, namely the German idealists, propagators of the (to him) ludicrous view that what is essential to concrete objects 'is not their actual, sensuously perceptible particular existence, but the essence I [the accused idealist] have abstracted from and substituted for them'.[30] Here Marxists might take comfort in the old saw that 'consistency is the vice of small minds'.[31]

We can plausibly argue, then, that Marx's denial of essen-

---

[29] 'On the Jewish Question', in *Writings of the Young Marx*, 241 (my emphasis). A few pages earlier, he grants that man 'is not yet an *actual* species-being' (231).

[30] *The Holy Family* (1845), in *Writings of the Young Marx*, 370.

[31] It should be clear that I disagree (or only half agree) with Norman Geras, who attempts to refute the 'legend' that Marx abandoned universalistic conceptions of human nature (see *Marx and Human Nature: Refutation of a*

tialist accounts of human nature refers only to the descriptive element—precisely the element that underpins the rights of man, which (like God's law) were presumed to have a real existence, irrespective of subjective moral preferences or perceptions. Needless to say, Marx recognizes that all human beings possess certain basic attributes—intentionality, language, tool-making—and he further assumes, perhaps wrongly, that these serve to distinguish us from the rest of the animal kingdom.[32] Beyond this bare minimum, however, the individual person is little more than a social cypher, a *tabula rasa*, whose psychology and defining traits are explained by his or her relationship to production. What human beings are, Marx insists, coincides with '*what* they produce and *how* they produce', and not with the timeless dictates of nature. For natural rights doctrine, in contrast, 'what men are' is determined by some innate property or properties—a human essence in the descriptive sense. Which brings us to Marx's main criticism of the 'rights of man': that their proponents confuse bourgeois man with man-in-general. The 'so-called rights of man' (life, liberty, property, security) are 'only the rights . . . of egoistic man, man separated from other men and from the community . . . man withdrawn into himself, his private interest and his private choice'. The idea of inviolable rights presupposes an atomistic conception where society 'appears to be an external framework for the individual, limiting his original independence'. In this impoverished vision, the 'only bond between men is natural necessity, need and private interest, the maintenance of their property and egoistic persons'.[33] Marx realized that inherent in the concept

---

Legend, London: Verso, 1983). The argument is set out with great rigour and ingenuity, but it surely goes too far and is difficult, if not impossible, to square with a central tenet of historical materialism: that 'what men are' is essentially determined by their particular mode of productive activity. From an exegetical point of view, this discrepancy seems an unacceptable price to pay. I believe that my own interpretation, while less exciting than the one advanced by Geras, rests upon the most natural reading of the ambiguous textual evidence. Nor does my account require me to claim, as does Geras, that Marx has been systematically misrepresented by scores, even hundreds, of commentators, many of them his devoted followers.

[32] Jon Elster argues persuasively that these characteristics are not unique to man. See *Making Sense of Marx* (Cambridge: Cambridge University Press, 1985), 62–8.

[33] 'On the Jewish Question', in *Writings of the Young Marx*, 235–7.

of natural rights is the assumption that, within certain spheres, collective needs must be subordinated to individual claims. This he was not prepared to accept. Nor was he willing to define freedom as a kind of sheltered garden, an *enclave* of individual autonomy in a web of social regulation. Hence his objection to the statement, contained in the French Declaration of the Rights of Man and of Citizens, that 'Liberty is the power belonging to each man to do anything which does not impair the rights of others'. In Marx's judgement, this 'is the liberty of man viewed as an isolated monad', pursuing personal gain in a context where all his relations with others are mediated by the market and commodity exchange. Liberty in this sense is based not 'on the association of man with man but rather on the separation of man from man. It is the *right* of this separation, the right of the *limited* individual limited to himself.'[34] Marx proceeds to make the following, very strange remark: 'The practical application of the right of liberty is the right of *private property*.' Note the use of the definite article: '*The* practical application...', not '*a* practical application'. For him, the individual liberty so dear to the hearts of bourgeois philosophers could have but one purpose—the protection of private property.[35] Such was the brutal logic of his economic reductionism.

Marx systematically discriminates between *political* eman-

---

[34] Ibid. 235. Marx acknowledges that at least some of the propositions or 'rights' listed in the French Declaration do not attach to individuals as such and therefore can hardly be attributed to 'egoistic man'. These rights, if that is what they are, seem to belong to the community as a whole. Marx, taking seriously the distinction made in the title of the Declaration, labels them the 'rights of citizens' (ibid. 233), as distinct from the 'rights of man'. Under this heading would come: Article III ('The nation is essentially the source of all sovereignty; nor can any individual, or any body of men, be entitled to any authority which is not expressly derived from it.'), Article XIII ('A common contribution being necessary for the support of the public force, and for defraying the other expenses of government, it ought to be divided equally among the members of the community, according to their abilities.'), Article XV ('Every community has a right to demand of all its agents, an account of their conduct.'), and Article XVI ('Every community in which a separation of powers and a security of rights is not provided for, wants a constitution.'). To those who accept the conventional view that universal rights, by definition, make claims on behalf of *individuals*, these propositions are not rights at all, but simply desirable principles of public life. In any case, Marx does not discuss them.

[35] Ibid. 235.

cipation, the 'reduction of man to a member of a civil society', and *human* emancipation, anchored in the idea of an integrated human being, in full control of his or her warring impulses. The former, bogus liberation produces a society of isolated, self-seeking individuals who see politics as the interplay of personal and sectional interests. The latter, 'true' liberation is achieved only 'when the actual, individual man has taken back into himself the abstract citizen and in his everyday life, his individual work, and his individual relationships has become a *species-being*'.[36] The inhabitants of bourgeois society, shattered and degraded by rotten institutions and practices, can discover their humanity only by recognizing themselves as bearers of the community, and by behaving accordingly. What Marx is arguing for is the perfect identity of particular and universal interests, that is, abolition of the liberal distinction between private and public. But, as he well understood, the purpose of natural and human rights doctrine is precisely to protect the citizen from such an identification, to remove certain spheres of action from the calculus of social utility.

Marx's ideal of liberation was poles apart from that of the Englightenment thinkers. Whereas they endeavoured, in the main, to free men from social pressure, to make them self-directing individuals, following their own inner light, Marx sought to enclose men within a tightly knit community, dedicated to a specific vision of human ends. The project of liberation, he wrote, is hopeless if confined to man 'just as he is, corrupted by the entire organisation of our society, lost and alienated from himself'. With reference to Englightenment achievements, Marx complained: 'man was not freed from religion; he received religious freedom. He was not freed from property. He received freedom of property.'[37] Stated otherwise, one does not liberate people by letting them speak freely, associate or worship as they please, dispose of their property or labour in accordance with their own wishes. This is illusory freedom, for these people would still be slaves to religion, property, and greed. Man's political emancipation, in

[36] Ibid. 241.
[37] Ibid. 231, 240.

the form of bourgeois rights, turns out to be 'the perfection of his slavery and his inhumanity'.[38] Authentic emancipation requires the remoulding of man in conformity to a particular pattern. Those who picture Marx as a child of the Enlightenment, wishing only to extend its achievements, seriously underestimate both the novelty and significance of his argument.

Marx's ferocious attack on human rights, set down in his early writings, was never modified, let alone abandoned, as he became older and wiser. But when returning to the subject years later he couched his objections in a sociological rather than philosophical idiom. Such rights were 'ideological nonsense' and 'obsolete verbal rubbish', reflecting the needs of a particular class and epoch.[39] Like all the rest of morality and metaphysics ('phantoms formed in the human brain'), human rights were 'necessary sublimations of man's material lifeprocess' and therefore devoid of even the semblance of independence or universality.[40] As Engels commented on the splendid ideals of the French Enlightenment, 'this kingdom of reason was nothing more than the idealized kingdom of the bourgeoisie'.[41]

---

[38] *The Holy Family*, in *Karl Marx: Selected Writings*, ed. and trans. D. McLellan (Oxford: Oxford University Press, 1977), 145. In order to forestall irrelevant criticism, it should be acknowledged that Marx, in 1842, did indeed attack censorship and defend freedom of the press in a series of articles for *Rheinische Zeitung*, a liberal bourgeois journal which he briefly edited. Censorship, he wrote, 'is a form of servitude, ... something purely negative'. A censored press is 'a thing without a backbone, a vampire of slavery, a civilized monstrosity, a scented freak of nature' (quoted in L. Kolakowski, *Main Currents of Marxism*, i, *The Founders* (Oxford: Oxford University Press, 1981) 121). At this stage, however, Marx was not yet a communist, and openly questioned the theoretical as well as practical validity of communist ideas. Instead, he could be described as a liberal or left-wing Hegelian, who presented an ideal of 'the state as the actualization of rational freedom', as a 'great organism' in which 'the individual citizen simply obeys the natural laws of his own reason' (*Writings of the Young Marx*, 128, 130, 134). This is precisely the kind of thinking that Marx, by 1843, came to disparage. *The Holy Family*, published in 1845, bore witness to his final break with the young Hegelian radicals who dominated *Rheinische Zeitung*. It is a virulent and sarcastic attack on his former allies and their absurd 'philosophical consciences'.

[39] 'Critique of the Gotha Program', in *Marx & Engels: Basic Writings*, 120.

[40] *The German Ideology*, in *Writings of the Young Marx*, 415.

[41] *Socialism: Utopian and Scientific*, in *Marx & Engels: Basic Writings*, 69.

What I have called Marx's philosophical critique of liberal democracy received little attention from the great Marxist thinkers who succeeded Marx himself. Most—Engels, Kautsky, Plekhanov, Lenin, Luxemburg—appeared to ignore it altogether. For a start, Marx's early works, where the critique is elaborated, were little known and much less read until after the Second World War. With few exceptions, they were published posthumously, some not until the 1920s and 1930s. Indeed, orthodox Marxists have always assumed that the young Marx, schooled in German philosophy, was still struggling to escape from the dark cave of idealism—hence his atavistic use of evaluative, unscientific terminology such as 'human nature' and 'alienation'. For classical Marxists, socialism was not the recovery by man of his lost humanity, the reconciliation of his essence with his empirical existence; rather, socialism was understood more practically, as the new system that would do away with inefficiency, exploitation, and social antagonism. The outstanding exception was Gyorgy Lukács, whose 'humanistic' interpretation of Marxist philosophy inspired later generations of Marxists and neo-Marxists. In his master-work, *History and Class Consciousness*, first published in 1921, he deliberately set out to develop certain key aspects of Marx's philosophical anthropology. The most noteworthy result was the Hungarian's famous doctrine of 'reification', which bears a close resemblance to political alienation as conceived by Marx. Put as simply as possible, reification is the condition whereby human society, the creation of man, appears not as the product of social activity, but as a nightmare of alien, impersonal forces, beyond human comprehension or control, which impose themselves on us from without. Human beings become objects, passive spectators of a process that structures their lives for them. This passivity, according to Lukács, is fostered by the pervasive differentiation of bourgeois life into separate and distinct spheres, thus leading to 'the destruction of every image of the whole'.[42] The pitiless advance of specialization, which begins in the factory but soon spreads like a disease to all parts of the

---

[42] *History and Class Consciousness*, trans. R. Livingstone (Cambridge, Mass.: MIT Press, 1971), 103.

social body, 'seems to penetrate the very depths of man's physical and psychic nature' and represents 'a violation of man's humanity', a grotesque fragmentation of the human personality.[43] While Lukács was primarily concerned with the degrading nature of work in the capitalist enterprise, he also maintained, following Marx, that bourgeois man is torn asunder by 'the abstract and absolute separation of the state from the economy'. And, like his mentor, he was also interested in the practical consequences of this separation: on the one hand, 'economic fatalism', a belief in the iron necessity of the laws of capitalism, and, on the other, 'ethical utopianism', a naïve faith in the power of politics to remedy the evils of the market.[44]

Lukács was pilloried by orthodox Marxists for having the temerity to stress the 'subjective factor' and for positing some natural human essence, struggling to express itself in history. The guardians of 'scientific' Marxism, backed by the authority and resources of the Kremlin, soon forced him to retract his proto-Hegelian philosophizing and managed to bury this heresy for some while. But a number of factors combined to resurrect the humanistic, moralistic critique of bourgeois society that shines through Marx's youthful reflections. Two seem most important. First, there was the failure of the revolution to materialize in any advanced capitalist state, despite the iron-clad guarantees offered by the materialist dialectic. It became clear to many Marxists that capitalism was not about to self-destruct purely on account of its inherent contradictions. Secondly, there was the evident failure of 'actually existing socialism' to build 'the realm of freedom' or anything like it. The feeling arose that human liberation could not be assured by the simple transfer of property ownership from private to public hands. Some Marxist philosophers thus turned their attention to the deficiencies of the theory in the field of ethics and ontology. Sociological and economic critiques of capitalism were regarded as insufficient; it was also necessary to protest against dehumaniza-

---

[43] Ibid. 99, 101.
[44] Ibid. 195–6.

tion and put forward an alternative concept of man and his place in the universe. The aim was to restate the old doctrine of personal salvation as a gospel of socialism.

Since the end of the Second World War, humanism has replaced 'scientism' as the dominant fashion amongst Marxist intellectuals, a number of whom have revived Lukács' idea of reification: the disintegration of human 'wholeness' and the subjection of man to alien, quasi-natural forces. Here we may single out two dynamic groups of Marxist (or neo-Marxist) theoreticians: the Frankfurt School, whose best known members were Herbert Marcuse, Max Horkheimer, and Theodor Adorno; and the Yugoslav thinkers associated with the journal *Praxis*, notably Mihailo Marković and Rudi Supek. The former group railed against the degradation of mass society, with its blind worship of technology and consumer goods and its profound indifference towards cultural or spiritual values. The Yugoslavs, for their part, interpreted Marx's attack on the alienating dualism of politics and economic life under capitalism as a justification for shop-floor democracy, an arrangement where workers in any given enterprise do not simply fulfil production norms imposed by the community (or, more accurately, the central planning authorities) but themselves decide all questions of production and distribution.[45] Worker self-autonomy at the point of production was, as we shall see more clearly in our next chapter, scorned by orthodox Marxists, whose model for the economy was a 'large engineering works',[46] with each individual part perfectly co-ordinated with the rest in the pursuit of common objectives.

Still, the contrast between 'humanistic' and 'scientific' Marxists should not be exaggerated, as certain elements of Marx's philosophical critique of bourgeois society have never been absent from the collective consciousness of *all* his followers. While the language of alienation may offend against the scientific sensibilities of some, Marxists uniformly condemn bourgeois individualism and particularly the 'dog-eat-dog' mentality of capitalism, though this condemnation

---

[45] See, for example, M. Marković, 'Socialism and Self-management', *Praxis*, 1 (1965).

[46] A. Gramsci, *Selections from Political Writings: 1910–1920*, ed. Q. Hoare and trans. J. Mathews (London: Lawrence and Wishart, 1977), 263.

may not be central to their analysis. There is also total agreement that the private/public split serves to depoliticize the key source of power: private ownership of the means of production. Economic power is treated as if it were not a proper subject of politics, because the massive division between those who own and control the productive forces and those who must live by their labour power is seen as the outcome of free private contracts. It would be hard, moreover, to find a Marxist who did not deplore the mass apathy generated by the bourgeois relegation of politics. One might suppose that Marx's eloquent dismissal of natural, or human, rights would also unite all tendencies within the broad Marxist church. Are these rights not logically bound up with bourgeois individualism and Christian essentialism? Somewhat surprisingly, no unanimity prevails on this matter. Here it is the humanists who are least likely to endorse Marx's position, though they often claim that the great prophet's teachings have been misunderstood. An argument commonly advanced is that Marx wished to denounce not human rights as such but their abstract or formal expression under capitalism, where they are restricted to a single sphere of activity—politics—and where their practical effect is virtually negated by inequalities of wealth and status. Listen to Ernst Bloch:

In his denunciation of private property as a bourgeois limitation upon the rights of man, did Marx reject freedom, the right of the people to resist oppression and to insure its own security? Not at all! Marx's aim, rather, was to carry the idea of freedom further, to develop its logical consequences freed from the checks and hindrances of private property and the latter's increasingly destructive incursions. He is so far from being a critic of freedom that, on the contrary, he views freedom as a glorious human right.[47]

Respect for human rights was a prominent theme amongst so-called Eurocommunists, who tried to promote the acceptable face of communism by singing the praises of parliamentary democracy. Santiago Carrillo, a major spokesman for the cause, believed he was 'remaining true to the essentials of revolutionary Marxism' when he took up the cudgels for 'a

[47] 'Man and Citizen According to Marx', in *Socialist Humanism*, ed. E. Fromm (New York: Doubleday, 1966), 224.

socialism which would maintain and enrich the democratic political liberties and human rights which are historic achievements of human progress'.[48] The challenge for Marxism, then, is not to destroy this heritage but to extend it. One doubts whether Marx would have agreed. It is indeed true that he decried the hypocrisy of those politicians and theorists who exalt the rights of man while at the same time defending unrestrained bourgeois tyranny in the economic sphere. And he certainly thought that even when the in-fluence of wealth, rank, and education is excluded officially from legal and political systems, pervasive and profound un-official influences still flourish.[49] But can we conclude that Marx was attacking not the very concept of human rights but simply the way those rights were expressed in bourgeois society? I think not. Allen Buchanan, one of the more rigorous analysts of Marx, makes a useful distinction between his internal and external critiques of rights theory. Some of Marx's criticisms 'are launched from a perspective within the conception of rights he is attacking, while others are ad-vanced from a vantage point which is external'.[50] Marx's main internal criticisms focus on the inadequacy of political emancipation because of the enduring inequalities of wealth, education, and occupational status. Marx's 'external' critique is more radical. When he declares that the rights of man are those of 'an isolated monad', 'separated from other men and from the community', his point is surely that such rights, by their very nature, apply to solitary and competitive persons, trapped in an exchange economy whose guiding ethos is mutual plunder and deceit. In a truly human, co-operative society, untainted by the adversarial spirit, these boundary markers would have no place. An individual would neither need nor want to assert his own exclusive interests against the community that nurtures him from cradle to grave. Only this interpretation, Buchanan argues, could explain why Marx

[48] *Eurocommunism and the State* (Westport, Conn.: Lawrence Hill, 1978), 12, 19.

[49] 'On the Jewish Question', in *Writings of the Young Marx*, 224–5.

[50] *Marx and Justice: The Radical Critique of Liberalism* (London: Methuen, 1982), 67. For a complementary and equally penetrating discussion of Marx on rights, see S. Lukes, *Marxism and Morality* (Oxford: Clarendon Press, 1985), 61–70.

nowhere even suggests that human liberation should be defined in terms of rights, however conceived.

In any case, the idea of eternal rights, discovered by the pure light of natural reason and attaching to man *qua* man, regardless of particular circumstances, is evidently invalidated by historical materialism. Near the turn of the century, however, a small group of Austrian Marxists, led by Otto Bauer, sought to refute this inference, claiming that scientific materialism must be complemented by universalistic and specifically Kantian ethics. As Bauer points out to his fellow Marxists, 'the recognition that socialism will come into existence does not yet lead me to fight for it. If we regard the social question no longer as a scientific issue, but as one involving a practical attitude, then it is certainly a moral question.' But it is not 'the business of science to make moral judgements'.[51] For these we must turn to Kant's ethic, which, according to Max Adler, represents an implicit 'philosophical expression of the human aims of socialism'. The categorical imperative, which embodies the concept of universal legislation, rules out the 'oppression of any willing subject'; while the requirement that every man should be treated as an end, rather than as a means, is 'an idea which excludes all exploitation'.[52] These 'neo-Kantians' found a formidable foe in Karl Kautsky, perhaps the most influential Marxist thinker of his time, who flatly denied the existence of 'a timeless and universal moral law residing in human beings by virtue of some supernatural realm'. Since historical materialism 'brings morality down to earth' from the 'heavenly heights', abstract moral idealism, he concluded, 'has no place in scientific socialism'.[53] The neo-Kantians were therefore engaged in a bizarre attempt to mix the theoretical equivalents of chalk and cheese.

But, as we have seen, Marx condemns more than the universalistic pretensions of human rights; he also objects to

[51] 'Marxism and Ethics', in *Austro-Marxism*, texts trans. and ed. T. Bottomore and P. Goode (Oxford: Clarendon Press, 1978), 81.

[52] 'The Relation of Marxism to Classical German Philosophy', in *Austro-Marxism*, 63.

[53] 'Marxism and Ethics', in *Karl Kautsky: Selected Political Writings*, ed. and trans. P. Goode (London: Macmillan 1983), 40–3.

their *content*. For these rights, as normally understood, are essentially *negative* rights, epitomized by 'the right to do and perform anything that does not harm others'.[54] The aim is to allow human agents to pursue their self-chosen goals in the absence of man-made constraints, whether these goals be misguided or laudable, selfish or altruistic. In Marx's opinion, this type of freedom was barely worth having: the 'rights of man', paradoxically, amounted to 'the perfection of his slavery'. This contempt for negative freedom has received concrete expression in every communist regime. Yet even some orthodox Marxists have betrayed unease when confronted by this particular aspect of Marx's critique of liberalism. Kautsky is one example—and he spoke for many during the early days of the movement. While unequivocally rejecting the idea of *natural* (i.e. timeless, universal) rights, he nevertheless regarded freedom of the spoken and written word, the right of assembly, and artistic freedom as automatic features of socialist organization. Although property rights were dispensable, the ultimate destination, to his mind, was not social ownership of the means of production, but abolition of every form of oppression. Imposing limits on free expression seemed an odd way to achieve this end. Negative freedom, shorn of its metaphysical trappings, was therefore an integral part of human liberation, not an optional extra—and certainly not a mere consequence of bourgeois selfishness.[55] Kautsky also put forward a utilitarian justification for free expression. In the manner of J. S. Mill, he believed that it would widen mental horizons and stimulate the growth of knowledge—both essential to the development of the 'new socialist man'. One could not produce this superior being by imitating the methods of the Spanish Inquisition, by attempting to control how people think and behave.[56]

Kautsky's defence of liberal freedoms was formulated in the course of his attack on the Bolshevik Revolution. Lenin, with characteristic vituperation, responded by describing

---

[54] 'On the Jewish Question', in *Writings of the Young Marx*, 235.

[55] *The Dictatorship of the Proletariat*, in *Karl Kautsky: Selected Political Writings*, 99–100.

[56] *Terrorism and Communism*, in *Karl Kautsky: Selected Political Writings*, 142–3.

the German as a 'lackey of the bourgeoisie', a 'parliamentary cretin', guilty of 'bottomless stupidity and philistinism' and incapable of grasping 'the fundamental principles of Marxism'. The rights eulogized by Kautsky were the ideological supports of the bourgeois system and had to be destroyed along with it. For Lenin, it was simply absurd to grant rights to the bourgeoisie and other counter-revolutionaries (a term he defined loosely). Those who thought otherwise were 'spineless hangers-on of the bourgeoisie ... drooping intellectuals', objective enemies of the people.[57]

Whatever one may think of Lenin's violent language (and actions) his root-and-branch denunciation of 'bourgeois rights' seems to tally with Marx's own position. All the same, such is the international prestige of 'human rights' that even Lenin's disciples frequently paid (and pay) lip-service to them, if only for propaganda purposes. Indeed, communist regimes regularly assured us of their commitment to such rights and even enshrined them in constitutions. The Soviet Constitution of 1977, to take the most prominent example, guaranteed freedom of speech, of the press, and of assembly, meetings, street processions, and demonstrations (Article 50); the right to associate in public organizations (Article 51); and freedom of conscience, that is, the right to profess any religion (Article 52). Article 56, in the land of the KGB, protected the privacy of correspondence and telephone conversations. These liberal provisions were, however, absurdly negated by Article 62: 'Citizens of the USSR are obliged to safeguard the interests of the Soviet state, and to enhance its power and prestige.'[58] Anyone prepared to detect ambiguity in this provision can turn, for illumination, to an official (pre-glasnost) publication which explains the rights and freedoms of the Soviet people. There we learn that 'freedom and socialist democracy are freedom for the whole people building a communist society

[57] V. I. Lenin, *The Proletarian Revolution and the Renegade Kautsky* (London: Martin Lawrence, 1935), 26, 24, 36, 60; and 'Fright at the Fall of the Old and the Fight for the New', Jan. 1918, in *The Lenin Anthology*, ed. R. Tucker (New York, W. W. Norton, 1975), 425.

[58] *Constitution (Fundamental Law) of the Union of Soviet Socialist Republics*, adopted in 1977 (Moscow: Novosti Press Agency Publishing House, 1977), 46–51.

rather than freedom for our adversaries [dissidents] to work against the socialist state'. The 'genuine freedom of man' is 'the freedom to act in the interests and for the lofty goals of society and freedom from all prejudices and class antagonisms'. If, as this quotation implies, genuine freedom presupposes conformity to socially defined roles and assumptions, then non-conformists are enslaved by their own defective outlook, and the authorities, armed with Article 62, can force these recalcitrants to be 'free', or 're-educate such people and prevent them from making mistakes'.[59] In practice, this meant that any Soviet citizen who publicly criticized official Soviet policy could, quite constitutionally, stand trial on charges of 'anti-Soviet slander'. It appears that everyone possessed freedom of expression—as long as he or she expressed the right thing.

In spite of surface appearances, Marx's 'external critique' of human rights doctrine informed Soviet constitutional theory, though Gorbachev and his supporters did exhibit great admiration for Kautsky's views on this matter. Glasnost harked back to the quasi-liberal strand in Marxist thought, especially evident in the years between Marx's death and the Bolshevik Revolution, but recently revived by the humanists and Eurocommunists. According to a *Pravda* editorial of 14 April 1988, democratic development 'is impossible without freedom of thought and word, without an open and broad clash of views'.[60] In a similar Millsian vein, Gorbachev himself told us that the search for truth 'must be carried out by counterposing various points of view, debates and discussions, breaking the old stereotypes'.[61] Diversity and free expression came to enjoy official favour; and yet the Soviet President could not avoid a certain ambivalence:

Life today convinces us ... that without a political *avant garde*, able ideologically and organisationally to unite the best forces of the country, to interpret [*osanyslit'*] the processes occurring in society, to put into effect the results of this scientific analysis—without such

[59] F. Medvedev and G. Kulikov, *Human Rights and Freedoms in the USSR*, trans. L. Lezhneva (Moscow: Progress Publishers, 1981), 190, 203–5.

[60] p. 2.

[61] *Pravda*, 2 Oct. 1986, p. 1.

an *avant garde*, that is without the communist party, no transformations will be possible ... We are for *glasnost'* without any reservations, without restrictions. *But for* glasnost' *in the interests of
socialism* ... if *glasnost'*, criticism, democracy are in the interests of
the people, then they have no limits![62]

While this statement no longer has any practical relevance,
it is nevertheless instructive, for it shows how the reforming
Soviet leader encountered the same theoretical difficulty that
bedevils all Marxists who express a willingness to modify
their collectivism in the name of negative freedom: to wit, if
one affirms the cognitive superiority of Marxism, which alone
avoids distortion of reality, what exactly is the justification
for free expression or any other negative right? Shouldn't
enlightened Marxist guardians simply guide us, with a firm
hand, along the path of truth? To Marx himself, the person
who 'freely' chooses to be a Christian or a Jew or an entrepreneur is not really free at all, for he or she is necessarily
imprisoned by false consciousness, itself the product of a
perverted environment. Freedom consists not in making
choices but in living in accordance with our 'rational' selves
and thereby attaining self-mastery. But then freedom from
external constraints would seem to be a contingent value,
worthwhile only if it leads to the right outcomes ('the interests of socialism'); it is not an integral component of human
liberation. Kautsky, for his part, saw no need to agonize over
these apparent inconsistencies in his argument. Given his
boundless faith in history's material laws, he took it for
granted that self-governing workers would, in a climate of free
debate, inevitably become Marxists. This bland assurance will
no longer do. Marxists are obliged to tell us whether they

---

[62] *Pravda*, 13 Jan. 1988, pp. 1–3 (my emphasis). This quotation, along with
the previous two, is cited by N. Lampert in 'The Dilemmas of *Glasnost*', *The
Journal of Communist Studies*, 4 (Dec. 1988), 49, 54–6. Lampert points out
that the Soviet press, in criticizing those responsible for inertia, mismanage-
ment, and corruption, was carrying out a time-honoured function of Soviet
journalism: to act as a collective 'propagandist, agitator, and organiser'
(Lenin's much quoted words) for the ruling party, defending the general
interest as currently defined by the political leadership against centrifugal
tendencies that seemed to defeat the intentions of the policy makers. In this
sense, the continuity between Gorbachev and his predecessors was greater
than some might think.

would support freedom of expression even when doing so would (or could) hinder or endanger the socialist cause. Marx himself offers no conceivable justification for such tolerance. On the contrary, he thought that negative freedom was wrong in principle. And his modern defenders, for all their philosophical sophistication, find it hard to combine, even rhetorically, their commitment to Marxism with a consistent commitment to personal freedom. Ernst Bloch, for example, after announcing that 'the rights to freedom of assembly, freedom of association, freedom of the press, and to individual security are today more important than ever', then says that, under socialism, these rights 'take on more positive meaning as rights to inexorably objective, practical criticisms for the furthering of socialist construction, within the framework of solidarity'.[63] What about the rights of those who do not wish to confine themselves to 'practical criticisms for the furthering of socialist construction'? On this Bloch is silent.

Among recent Marxists the Italian, Galvano della Volpe, has been most explicit in depicting negative freedom (*libertas minor* in his parlance) as specifically bourgeois, stemming from the simultaneous estrangement of people from each other and from the community. Expanding on Marx's early texts, della Volpe defines socialist liberty, or '*libertas maior*', as 'the right of everyone to *social* recognition of his personal qualities and capacities'.[64] Whatever the precise meaning of this formulation, *libertas maior* is obviously a 'positive' concept which, far from limiting public interference in the private lives of individuals, seems to presuppose it. Della Volpe has the merit of honestly presenting what we might call Marxism's primary view of negative freedom, or freedom of conscience, press, property, etc., as being essentially reducible to 'the right of the limited individual limited to himself'.[65] This view accords with Marx's 'external' critique of

---

[63] 'Man and Citizen According to Marx', in *Socialist Humanism*, 224–5.

[64] 'Comunismo e democrazia moderna', in *Rousseau e Marx* (Rome: Riuniti, 1957), 47–53.

[65] 'On the Jewish Question', in *Writings of the Young Marx*, 235. Della Volpe later revised his opinion somewhat, thus joining the ranks of the Marxist prevaricators. In 1965, for example, he conceded that 'the triumph of egalitarian liberty' (*libertas maior*) does not necessitate the total obliteration of *libertas minor*. Egalitarian liberty 'will transcend mere civil liberty', but

the 'so-called rights of man', which sees them as evincing an atomistic approach to human practice.

How sound is the Marxian critique of parliamentary democracy? Marx was right, I think, to highlight the inconsistency in liberal thinking between the desire for equality in the political realm and the acceptance of rigid hierarchy within the economic sphere. Why should democratic procedures be appropriate to one sphere but not the other? Liberal defenders of capitalism assume that economic power differs from political power in some crucial respect that justifies waiving the requirement of democratic accountability. Upon close inspection, however, the conceptual distinction between the two types of power seems to collapse. Even David Easton, an eminent *liberal* political scientist, defines 'political life' to include 'all those varieties of activity that influence significantly the kind of authoritative policy adopted for a society and the way it is put into practice'.[66] Under this by no means eccentric definition, it is reasonable to conclude that economic power is a sub-category of political power, for the heads of large corporations regularly and undeniably make authoritative decisions on matters—living standards, plant location, the magnitude and rate of technological innovation—that 'influence significantly' either the local community directly involved, or the country as a whole, or both. Big businessmen are political actors in all but name. What Marxists refer to as 'the dictatorship of capital' may be practical, insofar as it offers the most efficient route to economic well-being; but it is hard to see how it can be regarded as anything other than an affront to democratic values. It might, however, be objected that the free market, to which capitalists must respond, is itself a democratic institution, accurately reflecting the choices of each and every citizen in his or her capacity as consumer. But it requires no special insight to realize that

'transcend' in the Hegelian sense, which implies that 'mere civil liberty' will be absorbed as well as superseded in the socialist state. What he seems to mean is that civil liberties (negative freedoms mainly) are acceptable, even desirable, as long as they do not conflict with 'egalitarian liberty'. And where, in della Volpe's opinion, do we find this perfect harmony of *libertas minor* and *libertas maior*? In the Soviet Union, 'the liberator of the human race'. See 'The Legal Philosophy of Socialism', in *Socialist Humanism*, 436–8.

[66] *The Political System* (New York: Alfred A. Knopf, 1953), 128.

market power varies with wealth: there is no 'equality of citizenship' within the capitalist market.

Another possible rejoinder to my argument might run as follows: in a liberal political system, the state is the highest locus of power, other realms being both formally and substantively subsumed under its authority. If capitalists exert massive control over resources, human as well as physical, this is because the democratic electorate consents to this control, which it could diminish or eliminate through legislation if it so wished. Let us, for the moment, grant the basic and controversial premise of this argument. Let us assume (as no Marxist would) that in existing liberal democracies economic relations are ultimately accountable to the autonomously formulated preferences of the majority. The fact remains that on the micro-level, the level of everyday life, capitalists exercise power over the rest of us. Capitalist firms are structures of command and obedience: wage labourers must do as they are told by their superiors in the hierarchy. Decisions are grounded in profit-maximization rather than the wishes of the work-force or the surrounding community. These decisions can destroy our towns and our livelihoods, and the affected localities and individuals have little or no say in the matter. Whether or not society in some sense consents to this type of domination is largely irrelevant from a democratic viewpoint. A willing slave is still a slave; a popular dictatorship is still a dictatorship. Democracy and corporate capitalism are strange bedfellows, and those who try to justify the latter as a mechanism for ensuring the maximum diffusion of power leave themselves open to the charge of hypocrisy. The best way to rebut this charge would be to argue that political democracy, in the Western sense, could not survive in the absence of private property in the means of production, a natural bulwark against the concentration of power in state hands. Thus, in order to preserve such democracy as we have, we must reject communal systems of ownership, however democratic these might sound. For if we attempt to be too democratic we shall, ironically, end up being *un*democratic. Even if correct, this argument, which will be considered in a later chapter, falls short of addressing the substance of Marx's charge: that liberal democracy, in effect, confines equality of power to the narrowly political sphere, thereby ignoring a large (perhaps the major) area of power relations within society.

But Marx wanted more than economic democracy, or the extension of citizenship to the industrial sphere. His wish to overcome the separation between civil and political society involved another type of unity: the perfect unity of the personal and communal life of every individual, the internalized identity of each person with the social totality, so as to eliminate tensions between his personal aspirations and his social loyalties or obligations. Only this conscious absorption of the individual by society could produce integrated human beings, at one with themselves and their environment. Marx's ideal was a society of selfless, other-regarding agents, indifferent to sectional ties or private interests and eager to display communal solidarity. But, as Kolakowski points out, the complete unity of public and private life is incompatible with those differences of interest and value that are ineliminable features of modern social existence. What Marx wanted 'would presuppose an unprecedented moral revolution running against the whole course of the past history of culture'.[67] Like Hegel and the German idealists, he was haunted by the supposed 'wholeness' of Greek civic life; unlike them, however, he believed that a perfectly integrated community, enjoying an unmediated identification of the personal and the collective, could be re-created in the conditions of an advanced society, with its complex division of labour and irreversible commitment to individual self-expression and independence. This vision is Utopian.[68] Nor is it obviously

[67] L. Kolakowski, 'The Myth of Human Self-identity', in *The Socialist Idea*, ed. L. Kolakowski and S. Hampshire (London: Weidenfeld and Nicolson, 1974), 33.

[68] Mihaly Vajda puts the interesting case that it 'was not because of the backwardness of Russian conditions that it became impossible for established socialism to achieve what was hoped of it. And this is an extreme understatement. It was rather those "backward" Russian conditions themselves which made it possible to experiment with this sort of concept of socialism in the first place.' For fundamentalist Marxism, he argues, is entirely inapplicable to societies that have experienced the 'disintegration of closed communities' and the 'universalization of human contacts'. These consequences of industrial development mean that the majority of our relational contacts will inevitably be functional and impersonal, or alienated in the Marxist sense (*The State and Socialism* (London: Allison and Busby, 1981), 85–6, 95).

desirable, unless, with Marx, we make the a priori (and rather implausible) assumption that the pursuit of self- or group interest necessarily kills the co-operative spirit and precludes the attainment of inner harmony and fulfilment. The liberal distinction between public and private, while offensive to those who conceive society as an 'expressive totality', is peculiarly suited to a world where forms of self-concerned behaviour, and therefore disagreements over social goals, are inevitable. In such a world, the rights of man denigrated by Marx manifest not selfishness but a legitimate fear of state despotism (whether or not this despotism masquerades as the 'general will'). The demand to choose one's own course of action, free from external interference, reveals nothing more sinister than a desire to preserve personal identity amidst the myriad and conflicting pressures of modern life. What Marx terms selfishness can more sensitively be described as reluctance to sacrifice one's own conscience and fundamental interests at the altar of 'community' or 'nation', especially when these abstractions are defined without due regard for the diversity of values within society.

Misguided though it is, the standard Marxist analysis of negative freedom does possess a grain of truth. Individual actions, however self-regarding, do have a bearing upon the context in which other individuals form and pursue their purposes. 'No man is an island', to quote the poet John Donne. We cannot, moreover, ignore the cultural and environmental factors that help to shape individual choice—the 'hidden persuaders' that influence the way we define our interests. Liberals sometimes appear to forget that human agents are neither self-contained nor self-determined in the strict and proper sense of the term. But it is invalid to deduce from these truisms that the demand to be left alone is, in all circumstances, either meaningless or narrowly self-centred. Recognition of the inescapable social dimension of our existence does not oblige us to deny the presence (or value) of an inner psychological core that enables individuals to bring something distinctive to the social roles they play. Of course, such a denial *is* required if we hold, with Marx, that 'the nature of individuals . . . depends on the material conditions which determine their production' (see note 25 above). For him, as we shall see more clearly in our concluding chapter, the human personality is *wholly* constituted by 'the ensemble of social relationships'. By belittling the rights of man, Marx remained true to this holistic premise; for negative freedom— the absence of external constraints on behaviour—has no relevance in a world-view which dissolves the individual self in the conceptual equivalent of sulphuric acid. This 'deconstructive' notion of the self is counter-intuitive and cannot, in any case, be tested by normal empirical methods. Yet it lies at the heart of Marxist thought, which typically gives priority to general and abstract determinations over the particular traits and desires of individuals. No one should be surprised if this philosophical holism translates into a sort of political holism where the individual person effectively vanishes in a concrete realization of some predefined 'Humanity'.

Marx himself never spelled out the practical implications of his belief that true freedom entails 'rational' behaviour rather than simply doing as one pleases. This was left to his later disciples. Consider the words of Herbert Marcuse, a prophet of the New Left in the 1960s:

The range of choice open to the individual is not the decisive factor in determining the degree of human freedom, but *what* can be chosen and what *is* chosen by the individual.... Free election of masters does not abolish the master or the slaves. Free choice among a wide variety of goods and services does not signify freedom if these goods and services sustain social controls over a life of toil and fear.[69]

It is the old Marxist story: free choice is valuable (and truly free) only when the correct things are being chosen. Marcuse does not fight shy of the consequences: 'Universal toleration becomes questionable when ... tolerance is administered to manipulated and indoctrinated individuals who parrot, as their own, the opinions of their masters, ...' Then, drawing the conclusion for which he has become notorious, he calls for:

the withdrawal of toleration of speech and assembly from groups and movements which promote aggressive policies, armaments,

---

[69] *One-Dimensional Man* (London: Sphere Books, 1972), 21.

chauvinism, discrimination on the grounds of race or religion, or which oppose the extension of public services, social security, medical care, etc. Moreover the restoration of freedom of thought may necessitate new and rigid restrictions on teaching and practices in the educational institutions which, by their very methods and concepts, serve to enclose the mind within the established universe of discourse and behaviour.[70]

Marcuse is not to every Marxist's taste, but his position does seem a valid inference from Marx's own views on rights and freedom. Note that Marcuse is not merely saying that the obstacles to human freedom may be internal as well as legal, that propaganda or uncritical socialization or irrational fantasies may limit our freedom as surely as repressive laws do. Echoing Marx, he is making the further and much more controversial point that self-determining or autonomous agents are bound to converge on a single form of life. This is why Marx can confidently proclaim that what a liberal regards as political emancipation is really 'the perfection of his slavery'. Marx thinks he has discovered how to realize our distinctive human powers, our 'species' essence. But 'man' is a complicated being, who cannot be encapsulated by some simple formula which owes more to metaphysical speculation than empirical analysis. Human potentialities are manifold and often contradictory, yet Marx gives no convincing reason why we should maximize his preferred ones rather than others. The components of human flourishing are sufficiently various to allow for many definitions of the 'good life' or the 'good person'. A strength of liberal democracy is its ability to accommodate this inherent diversity. Marx's vision of all-embracing communal solidarity, where each individual identifies his own welfare with that of his fellow citizens, is just one ideal amongst others. It enjoys no scientific status, and it cannot plausibly be described as more natural than the alternatives. Nostalgic for the expressive wholeness of simpler times, Marxism seeks to impose unjustifiable limits on human imagination, and prescribes for mankind with unfounded arrogance. The link between this prescription and

---

[70] 'Repressive Tolerance', in *A Critique of Pure Tolerance*, ed. R. P. Wolff *et al.* (Boston: Beacon Press, 1967), 90, 100–1.

communist totalitarianism will be further explored in my final chapter.

III   Sociological Critique

Crudely summarized, Marxism's philosophical critique of the bourgeois state treats it as an abstract system of political domination which denies the social nature of human beings and alienates them from genuine involvement in political life. We now turn to the sociological critique developed by Marx and his followers. As we have already seen, he rejected the Hegelian notion that the state was the 'realization of the ethical idea' or 'the image of reason'. For him, the state was not an independent public power acting for the public; it was, rather, a product of irreconcilable class antagonisms, working to sustain the privileges of those with property. Still, his account of the relation between classes and the state is not entirely free of ambiguity and comprises at least two strands: did he believe that the state was partially autonomous with respect to class interests, or entirely reducible to them?

When presenting his views in formulaic terms, Marx, like his partner Engels, reduced the liberal state to its capitalist or economic essence, in spite of the other social functions it performs. Let us call this the reductionist model, according to which liberal democracy, in common with all previous state forms, is nothing else than an instrument of class oppression, designed to reproduce the system of exploitation. In the *Communist Manifesto*, for example, we are bluntly told that 'the executive of the modern state is but a committee for managing the common affairs of the whole bourgeoisie', since 'political power, properly so-called, is merely the organized power of one class for oppressing another'.[71] Throughout history, each method of production gave rise to an appropriate political organization furthering the interests of the economically dominant class. The large-scale industry and universal competition of modern capitalism created their own political

---

[71] *Manifesto of the Communist Party*, in *Marx & Engels: Basic Writings*, 9, 29.

set-up, the democratic republic: 'the unlimited despotism of one class over other classes',[72] 'an instrument of exploitation of wage labor by capital',[73] 'a machine for the oppression of one class by another'.[74] On this view, the liberal representative state serves its essential purpose by repressing threats from subordinate groups or classes (e.g. by the use of police and army to break strikes), by providing services to individual capitalists (energy resources, roads, railways, subsidies), by arbitrating disputes between capitalists, by preventing unpredictable market fluctuations, and by securing foreign markets, through either diplomacy or military intervention. No one, Marx warns, should be fooled by the presence of elected parliaments, for these are 'part of the horrid machinery of class domination'. Universal suffrage is a 'sleight of hand' by the powers that be and is 'only employed by the people to sanction (choose the instruments of) parliamentary class rule once in many years'. Elections, along with parliamentary business, are controlled by state bureaucrats and professional politicians, a remote caste of 'stateparasites, richly paid sycophants and sincecurists', who—pockets bulging with loot from their capitalist paymasters—set themselves up as 'haughteous masters of the people'. It is therefore ridiculous for the masses to contemplate a parliamentary road to socialism: 'The political instrument of their enslavement cannot serve as the political instrument of their emancipation.'[75]

This reductionist approach was memorably developed by Lenin, who dismissed bourgeois democracy as 'restricted, truncated, false and hypocritical, a paradise for the rich and a trap and a snare and a deception for the exploited, for the poor'. Liberal rights are 'purely formal', for two basic reasons. First, the 'real business' of the state goes on in the bureaucracy rather than in parliament. The state apparatuses—military, police, civilian—function as a more or less unitary body

[72] K. Marx, *Eighteenth Brumaire of Louis Bonaparte*, in *Marx & Engels: Basic Writings*, 329.

[73] F. Engels, *The Origin of the Family, Private Property, and the State*, in *Marx & Engels: Basic Writings*, 392.

[74] F. Engels, 'Introduction' to K. Marx, *The Civil War in France* (Peking: Foreign Languages Press, 1970), 17.

[75] Ibid. 166-71, 228.

in the interests of the ruling class. Second, in capitalist society the conditions of electoral struggle are fundamentally distorted by money and property, bourgeois control of the media and meeting places, and so on.[76] Despite constitutional niceties, the liberal regime is 'venal and rotten',[77] 'a dictatorship of the filthy and self-seeking exploiters who are sucking the blood of the people'.[78] Freedom under capitalism amounts to 'freedom for the slave owners'.[79] My exposition here would be less than complete without the inclusion of Lenin's most famous words on the subject: 'To decide once every few years which member of the ruling class is to repress and crush the people through parliament—this is the real essence of bourgeois parliamentarism.'[80]

Few classical Marxist thinkers dissented from Lenin's basic analysis. Rosa Luxemburg, for example, described 'the present state' as 'an organization of the ruling class'. In other words, 'representative institutions, democratic in form, are in content the instruments of the interests of the ruling class'.[81] Hegelian Marxists were not immune to this class reductionism. Even Lukács, perhaps in contradiction to his strictures against 'vulgar' materialism, dismissed the rule of law as 'the brutal power instrument of capitalist oppression'.[82] The reductionist model could be taken to imply that the state is a pure epiphenomenon of the economic base, with no reciprocal effectivity, and that there is a perfect correspondence between base and superstructure. The liberal republic is thus seen as the archetypal form of bourgeois rule, 'hemmed in by the narrow limits set by capitalist exploitation' and consequently 'a democracy for the minority, only for the propertied classes, only for the rich'.[83]

This type of analysis is today most faithfully represented by the 'state monopoly capitalism' school of thought, otherwise known as STAMOCAP, which holds that monopoly forces

---

[76] *The Proletarian Revolution and the Renegade Kautsky*, 26–31.
[77] *The State and Revolution* (Moscow: Progress Publishers, 1949), 45.
[78] *The Proletarian Revolution and the Renegade Kautsky*, 55.
[79] *The State and Revolution*, 79.
[80] Ibid. 43.
[81] *Reform or Revolution* (New York: Pathfinder Press, 1970), 25, 28.
[82] *History and Class Consciousness*, 265.
[83] V. I. Lenin, *The State and Revolution*, 79.

have fused with the bourgeois state to form a single, monstrous mechanism of economic exploitation and political oppression, the sole aim of which is the reproduction of capitalism. This phase of development, unlike earlier stages when private property was genuinely private, requires extensive state intervention to provide credit and subsidies, regulate levels of exploitation and demand, and generally foster the conditions of capital expansion. With scant regard for verbal originality, two typical representatives of STAMOCAP thinking describe state power as 'an instrument of class oppression', superficial democratic appearances notwithstanding.[84] From this perspective, the bourgeoisie resembles the fox which, according to fable, transmutes defeat into an act of the highest wisdom. All the victories gained through the blood, sweat, and tears of the workers—from the right to strike to universal suffrage, from welfare legislation to factory acts—are interpreted as adept moves by the wily capitalists to retain their power.

The recently fashionable *staatsableitung* school, in its less sophisticated variants at any rate, also understands the representative state purely in terms of its functional capacity to recreate the capitalist mode of production. This approach involves the attempt logically to deduce the forms and purposes of bourgeois democracy from abstract principles of political economy: the nature of the wage relation, the processes of commodity circulation or capital accumulation. According to Elmar Altvater, for example, certain preconditions for the overall reproduction of 'capital in general' cannot be secured through the actions of its constituent units ('particular capitals'), because competitive pressures render such actions unprofitable. Logic therefore dictates the necessity of an 'ideal collective capitalist', the bourgeois state, which must supply infrastructure, maintain a legal order, regulate the labour market, and promote the interests of national capital in the

---

[84] A. Dragstedt and C. Slaughter, *State, Power and Bureaucracy* (London: New Park Publications, 1981), 25. For an authoritative survey of STAMOCAP theory, see B. Jessop, *The Capitalist State* (Oxford: Martin Robertson, 1982), 32–63. Jessop is a tireless and fastidious guide to the vast profusion of Marxist 'discourse' on 'the capitalist state', though he does, I think, tend to treat these often vapid outpourings with more solemnity than they deserve.

world market. The state, on this interpretation, is not so much an 'instrument', cynically manipulated by bourgeois exploiters, as an essential expression of certain functional needs in the perpetuation of capitalism. It is, to be sure, an 'executive committee' of the ruling economic class, though, like all executive committees, it must often take decisions that upset those sectors of the membership who are blinded by their immediate self-interest. Underlying the logical rigour and abstruse formulations of capital-logic analysis is a simple Marxist-Leninist axiom: the liberal state is nothing but a class state, 'expressing the general interests of capital'.[85] As one critical commentator observes, state institutions are reduced to 'mere filters through which the logic of capitalism is translated into legislation'.[86] They exist for the sole purpose of maintaining bourgeois domination, by force if necessary.

The reductionist model, whatever its precise form, rests upon a number of scarcely plausible assumptions, all of them difficult to reconcile with our experience: (i) that the agencies of socialization are monolithic in their ideological orientation; (ii) that the various state apparatuses are little more than the hired servants of the business/financial élite and pursue no corporate interests of their own; and (iii) that elected parliaments are mere 'talking shops', with no effective power to respond to democratic forces or to enact policies inimical to bourgeois interests. But if the classical Marxian view of 'bourgeois' democracy makes little contact with empirical reality, how do we account for its persistence? The answer is that Marxist political analysis is informed by a *prior* theory, historical materialism, according to which the basic purpose of the political/ideological superstructure is to preserve ('reproduce', in the current jargon) the existing set of economic relations. 'In the final analysis' (Engels's phrase), the political domain is determined by hidden economic pressures. Those who hold sway within the mode of production will also control the modes of political activity and their outcomes. Analysts who invoke this brand of economic reductionism

---

[85] E. Altvater, 'Notes on Some Problems of State Intervention', *Kapitalistate*, 1 (1973), 96–108.

[86] L. Johnston, *Marxism, Class Analysis and Socialist Pluralism* (London: Allen & Unwin, 1986), 70.

can always 'explain away' contrary evidence by reference to false consciousness, real interests, hidden conspiracies, etc. But such explanations are themselves validated by the theory, not by observed facts. The imagery of economic determination simply *rules out* the specificity and independence of particular political forces and struggles. What we have here is an antecedent theoretical commitment, in no obvious way verified by historical experience. It is ironic that Marxists, for all their criticisms of German speculative philosophy, often display the Hegelian tendency to make deductions about social conditions from abstract schemes, with insufficient regard for the evidence of our senses.

Yet the Marxist tradition has not been entirely consistent or emphatic in its dismissal of 'bourgeois' democracy. On the one hand, there is the view we have just outlined: that parliament and liberal political rights are peculiarly suited to the interests of the bourgeoisie; on the other, we find the belief or recognition that the democratic republic embodies practices and values that can be used *against* the bourgeoisie and even undermine their supremacy. In discussing the rise of Louis Bonaparte, for example, Marx writes: 'The bourgeoisie had a true insight into the fact that all the weapons which it had forged against feudalism turned their points against itself.... It understood that all the so-called bourgeois liberties and organs of progress attacked and menaced its *class rule*.'[87] Kautsky was a firm advocate of this opinion. For him, freedom of speech, of the press, and of assembly were not empty bourgeois phrases; they were, on the contrary, 'the light and air of the labour movement', allowing the proletariat to 'exercise an influence over the governmental powers'. Parliament thus 'ceases to be a mere tool in the hands of the bourgeoisie'.[88] According to this view, the representative state is not now, nor has it ever been, a neutral arbiter, above the class battle; but neither must it always, and in all circumstances, obey the commands or further the interests of the bourgeoisie.

---

[87] *The Eighteenth Brumaire of Louis Bonaparte*, in *Marx & Engels: Basic Writings*, 332.

[88] *The Class Struggle*, trans. W. E. Bohn (New York: W. W. Norton, 1971), 184–8.

Notwithstanding his more rigid formulations, Marx (and later Marxists) conceded that the state, and not just its liberal variant, could enjoy a certain ('relative') autonomy. This flexible approach was especially evident when he was considering actual historical events. He even suggested that the French state under Louis Bonaparte had 'made itself *completely independent*', because of the peculiar balance of social forces, with the economic élite divided and the proletariat still too weak to destroy it.[89] Engels provided a neat theoretical proposition to cover such cases:

By way of exception ... periods occur in which the warring classes balance each other so nearly that the state power, as ostensible mediator, acquires, for the moment, a certain degree of independence of both. Such was the absolute monarchy of the seventeenth and eighteenth centuries, which held the balance between the nobility and the class of burghers; such was the Bonapartism of the first, and still more of the second French empire, which played off the proletariat against the bourgeoisie and the bourgeoisie against the proletariat. The latest performance of this kind, in which ruler and ruled appear equally ridiculous, is the new German Empire of the Bismarck nation: here capitalists and workers are balanced against each other and equally cheated for the benefit of the impoverished Prussian cabbage *Junkers*.[90]

The state thus asserts itself by the process of 'divide-and-conquer'. Marx and Engels understood, even if Lenin did not, that bureaucrats, judges, and politicians develop distinctive personal and professional interests, which may, in given situations, cause them to side with the exploited against the exploiters. That is, the political and legal powers of the state may develop an integrity and logic of their own. Even then, however, the state, if not actually an *instrument* of class oppression, is still a *condition* of this oppression, for it must, in the end, preserve law and order. Louis Bonaparte, for instance, under whom business and trade prospered 'in hothouse fashion', served to rescue the bourgeoisie from its own

[89] *The Eighteenth Brumaire of Louis Bonaparte*, in *Marx & Engels: Basic Writings*, 337 (my emphasis). Could Marx really mean *completely* independent? It is more likely that he got carried away by his own rhetoric.

[90] *The Origin of the Family, Private Property and the State*, in *Marx & Engels: Basic Writings*, 392–3.

political incompetence during the heady days of the second French Republic (1848–51). Disorganized, riddled with anxieties about the vestigial power of the aristocracy and the increasing demands of the emergent proletariat, the bourgeoisie floundered perilously in the parliamentary arena and finally realized that 'in order to save its purse it must forfeit the crown'. Power was ceded to a strong man who, by destroying parliament, delivered the exploiting class from the dangers of its own political rule. While Bonaparte took orders from no one, and loudly proclaimed his affinity with the humble folk, he nevertheless guaranteed an orderly climate for capitalist development.[91]

What Marx and Engels seem to be saying is this: in situations of class balance or stalemate, the state exhibits a relative autonomy, but ultimately its privileges are bound up with those of the dominant economic class, whose interests it promotes indirectly, through the maintenance of social and economic stability. Were the state to undermine the process of capital accumulation it would simultaneously undermine the material basis of its own existence. So the state can satisfy the objective needs of the bourgeoisie without being the direct extension of its subjective will. But, as Engels points out, this is the 'exception' not the rule. Where the capitalists are strong and united, they can expect to control the democratic republic through their political and bureaucratic henchmen. However, where the capitalists are weak or divided, the state will display a *relative* autonomy.

In recent years, many Marxist theoreticians have tended to favour this more flexible formulation of determination *in the last instance* when dealing with the 'capitalist state', and they usually insist, often to the point of heresy, that some features of political life cannot be derived from class interest or economic needs. Their principal source of inspiration is Antonio Gramsci, a resolute foe of Marxist orthodoxy who challenged the epiphenomenal view of the state while reflecting on the world from a fascist prison cell. Deeply influenced by Hegelian thought, he ridiculed his fellow Marxists for

---

[91] *The Eighteenth Brumaire of Louis Bonaparte*, in *Marx & Engels: Basic Writings*, 346, 333.

interpreting the base/superstructure distinction as a linear, mechanical relationship between source and reflection or cause and effect. Although, in his celebrated *Prison Note-books*, he still saw the state as an organ of class domination, he nevertheless stressed that one could not reduce all questions of political practice to those of economics. For political activity, while arising from 'the terrain of economic life', also 'transcends it, bringing into play emotions and aspirations in whose incandescent atmosphere' all calculations 'obey different laws from those of individual profit'. Politics, in other words, exhibits distinctive principles and imperatives that are independent of economic pressures: 'many political acts are due to internal necessities of an organisational character, that is they are tied to the need to give coherence to a party, a group, a society'.[92]

More recently, Louis Althusser, the founder of 'structuralist' Marxism, has also rejected the crude economic determinism that underlies the reductionist model of the state. While criticizing Gramsci's Hegelian emphasis on human subjectivity, he agrees that social causation is complex and multiple. The different social 'structures', or practices, including the state, occupy 'differential times': each is relatively autonomous from the others, obeying its own logic, its own rhythms or patterns of development. Economic and political life are not related as cause and effect, but constitute an articulated combination, a structural whole, in which each presupposes and maintains the other, although economic factors are always determinant 'in the last instance'.[93]

Althusser confined himself to notoriously vague generalities. His most influential disciple, Nicos Poulantzas, has tried to put some flesh on the bones of his mentor's abstract discourse. In his opinion, the state cannot be controlled by an economically dominant bourgeoisie, since this class, subject as it is to competitive pressures and differences of immediate interest, constantly divides into 'fractions'. The structurally determined role of the capitalist state is to protect the long-

---

[92] *Selections from the Prison Notebooks*, ed. and trans. Q. Hoare and G. Nowell Smith (London: Lawrence and Wishart, 1971), 140, 408.
[93] *For Marx*, 89–128.

term interests of this fragmented and squabbling bourgeoisie, but the state can sustain this function only if it possesses a considerable degree of autonomy from the diverse fractions within the economic 'power bloc'. The main task is to preserve social cohesion, which requires the state to reconcile and co-opt a wide variety of social forces, including 'fractions' of the working class itself. By thus defusing popular militancy, the state ('the factor of cohesion of a social formation')[94] 'reproduces' the mode of production and therefore furthers the interests of those who benefit from the capitalist system. Nevertheless, because the relatively autonomous state gauges and responds to the balance of class forces, it often makes material concessions to working-class and other popular struggles, usually in the teeth of bourgeois hostility, though, to repeat, state intervention always tends to the stabilization of the *status quo*. The state, then, is neither an instrument to be possessed and wielded by a class nor a disinterested umpire seeking impartial solutions. Rather, it is a quasi-independent 'practice', operating within a set of functional imperatives or constraints whose purpose is to ensure that public policy supports the maintenance and future development of capitalism. In short, the liberal state acts on *behalf* of the exploiting class rather than at its *behest*. On this functional explanation, governmental and legal–administrative institutions are necessarily moulded in forms which optimally sustain capital accumulation, whether or not they pursue this end directly, and irrespective of the substantial reforms conceded to the dominated classes. In common with Althusser, Poulantzas insists on the 'specific effectivity' of political practice, and yet he allows that, in a qualified sense, it is class-reducible, which is why the liberal state is a *capitalist* state: 'by state power one can only mean the power of certain classes to whose interests the state corresponds.'[95] Whatever autonomy the state enjoys is circumscribed in the long run by the parameters of class-based power.

[94] 'The Problem of the Capitalist State', in *Ideology in Social Science*, ed. R. Blackburn (London: Fontana, 1972), 246. See also N. Poulantzas, *Political Power and Social Classes* (London: New Left Books, 1973), 287–8 and 331–40 in particular.

[95] 'The Capitalist State: A Reply to Miliband and Laclau', *New Left Review*, 95 (1976), 73.

We must now consider whether the Marxian view becomes more acceptable when presented in this modified version. Poulantzas (if we may take him as representative) assumes that everything the 'capitalist state' does contributes to social cohesion and therefore the survival of the capitalist mode of production. Here he commits an error common to functional analysis: he does not specify any criteria for deciding whether a practice or policy is functional to the system in question, apart from the fact that it actually occurs. Whether the state does X or not-X, it is preserving the capitalist order, for this is what it is programmed (by whom or what?) to do. This line of argument, being immune to any conflicting evidence, has understandably been dismissed as vacuous. Any state that falls short of initiating a revolution against capital is a 'capitalist state', no matter how friendly it might be to working-class interests. Perhaps, however, this proposition is less empty than it appears at first glance. States do, after all, maintain law and order, and the preservation of social order is more valuable to the 'haves' than to the 'have-nots' or 'have-littles'. Where the system generates inequalities of power and property, enforcement of the rules of social intercourse ('the factor of cohesion') will not benefit all citizens equally. It is also undeniable that the modern liberal state intervenes directly to facilitate the process of capital accumulation, regardless of which party is in power. Unpredictable and damaging market fluctuations are curbed either by control of money flow (taxation, public investment, subsidies) or by direct state purchase (e.g. military spending). All this is obvious enough and would hardly be denied by the most ardent defender of capitalism. Less obvious but also true is the proposition, meticulously argued by Charles Lindblom (himself a non-Marxist), that business enjoys a privileged position within the liberal political system, giving it disproportionate influence in comparison with other social interests, labour included. He cites two reasons for this. First, the private enterprise system allows corporate élites to make a variety of decisions—on the allocation of labour and natural resources, on plant location and technology to be used in production, indeed on every major aspect of production and distribution—that are of immense importance to the welfare of society. Businessmen thus become *de facto* public officials and exercise what are in truth public functions: 'jobs, prices, production, growth, the standard of living, and the economic security of everyone all rest in their hands'. A major role of government, therefore, is to see that businessmen carry out their tasks effectively. While I regret leaning so heavily on quotations, Lindblom presents his case with exemplary clarity and is worth quoting at length:

> government responsibility for avoiding inflation and unemployment is a common issue in elections. In all market oriented systems, a major concern of tax and monetary policy is their effects on business activity. In subsidies and other help to water, rail, highway, and air transport; in patent protection; in fair trade regulation; in tariff policy; in overseas trade promotion through foreign ministries; in subsidized research and development . . . in countless ways governments in these systems recognize that businessmen need to be encouraged to perform. . . . In the eyes of government officials, therefore, businessmen do not appear simply as the representatives of a special interest, as representatives of interest groups do. They appear as functionaries performing functions that government officials regard as indispensable. When a government official asks himself whether business needs a tax reduction, he knows he is asking a question about the welfare of the whole society and not simply about a favour to a segment of the population, which is what is typically at stake when he asks himself whether he should respond to an interest group.
>
> Any government official who understands the requirements of his position and the responsibilities that market-oriented systems throw on businessmen will therefore grant them a privileged position. He does not have to be bribed, duped, or pressured to do so. Nor does he have to be an uncritical admirer of businessmen to do so. He simply understands, as is plain to see, that public affairs in market-oriented systems are in the hands of two groups of leaders, government and business, who must collaborate and that to make the system work government leadership must often defer to business leadership. . . . To understand the peculiar character of politics in market-oriented systems requires . . . no conspiracy theory of politics, no theory of common social origins uniting government and business officials, no crude allegation of a power elite established by clandestine forces. Business simply needs inducements, hence a privileged position in government and politics, if it is to do its job.[96]

[96] *Politics and Markets* (New York: Basic Books, 1977), 172–3, 175.

This 'privileged position' does not preclude the possibility of conflict between business and government, or of business defeats. Businessmen 'ask for a great deal' and 'routinely protest any proposal to reduce any of their privileges', but disputes between the two spheres rarely question 'the fundamentals of their symbiotic relationship' and usually concern 'secondary issues', such as tax rates and particulars of regulation.[97] ('Secondary' does not of course mean 'trivial'.)

Lindblom's second reason for the supremacy of business is the phenomenon of 'circularity', whereby corporations and their apologists systematically influence the preferences and evaluations of ordinary citizens and effectively establish boundaries of public discussion. In the Western democracies, Lindblom asserts, 'core beliefs are the product of a rigged, lop-sided competition of ideas'.[98] The instruments of circularity are chiefly the mass media (typically owned by wealthy tycoons or corporations), business domination of voluntary associations, plus the deference of politicians and political parties towards corporate interests. The point is not that anti-capitalist ideas are suppressed or denied a hearing; it is that the complex and ubiquitous mechanisms of socialization overwhelmingly reinforce the *status quo*, making it unlikely that a majority of voters will favour (or even consider) policies antagonistic to the basic interests of capitalism. In Lindblom's words, 'processes of critical judgment are short-circuited', as capitalism is made to seem not just desirable but somehow *natural*.[99]

Do all these arguments, if granted, mean that the Marxists—or at least those of the 'relative autonomy' school—are right about the 'capitalist state'? Unkind followers of Marx might accuse Lindblom of reinventing the wheel, for his discoveries hardly come as news to them. Note, however, that for him the ballot box is not a sham: 'popular control is crippled though not paralyzed'.[100] This statement would certainly serve to distinguish him from the more hard-line Marxists who (following in Lenin's footsteps) proudly display their

---

[97] Ibid. 179–80.
[98] Ibid. 212.
[99] Ibid. 207.
[100] Ibid. 230.

contempt for 'parliamentary cretinism'. But what about the advocates of a parliamentary road to socialism? The belief that 'revolution' can come about through the ballot box boasts a distinguished pedigree. Marx himself, in an oft-cited speech, conceded that in countries with deep-rooted liberal traditions, peaceful means could *possibly* work, though this remark was untypical.[101] The first consistent exponent of a pacific path was Kautsky, the scourge of all those who would dismiss parliament as a 'useless ornament'. In his estimation, universal suffrage, if diligently exploited by the working class, would eventually make the state into an expression of the popular will. He was most unimpressed by the Leninist argument that parliament is a mere talking shop and that the real business of the state goes on behind the scenes. As he points out, if the proletariat reaches the stage where it becomes able through numbers and organizational strength to win a parliamentary majority, then this will betoken a profound change in public consciousness, making it very difficult for the capitalists to thwart mass opinion or manipulate the state apparatus in their favour. In any case, there is no objective reason why ordinary soldiers or policemen or civil servants should wish to oppose socialism, especially when this new system promises to raise the living standards of the entire community.[102]

Kautsky's ideas have been enthusiastically adopted by the Eurocommunists, tireless champions of a 'peaceful, democratic, legal, and gradual' transformation.[103] Still, for Kautsky and his recent followers, the liberal state remains effectively a 'tool of class rule', 'a capitalist institution', until the working people manage to gain control of it.[104] Here is where all Marxists differ from Lindblom. Nowhere does he identify the liberal state as a capitalist state. Nowhere does he say that the liberal body-politic operates exclusively in the interests of the dominant economic groups, that it is (in the hackneyed words

---

[101] 'Amsterdam Speech', in *The Marx–Engels Reader*, ed. R. Tucker (New York: W. W. Norton, 1972), 523.

[102] *The Dictatorship of the Proletariat*, in *Karl Kautsky: Selected Political Writings*, 101.

[103] J. Elleinstein, 'The Skein of History Unrolled Backwards', in *Eurocommunism*, ed. G. R. Urban (London: Maurice Temple Smith, 1978), 88.

[104] K. Kautsky, *The Class Struggle*, 105, 110.

of Santiago Carrillo) 'the instrument of class domination'.[105] To Lindblom, the 'symbiotic relationship' between government and business persists only because, ultimately, capitalism succeeds in 'delivering the goods' to the population at large. In contrast, when Marxists argue that the 'bourgeois' state reflects the interests of the business/financial élite, they smuggle in the dubious assumption that the mass of ordinary people would be materially better off under an alternative (socialist) set of social arrangements. While this *may* be true (how does one disprove a counterfactual statement?), the available evidence would seem to support the opposite proposition. One need only consider the pathetic queues outside shops and restaurants that disfigured the daily lives of ordinary citizens in the resource-rich Soviet Union. Less impressionistically, one could point to the undignified retreat from Marxist economics throughout the communist (and former communist) world, where market forces and private enterprise are being hailed as solutions to years of economic stagnation. The structural weaknesses of socialist planning are well known and barely need rehearsing here.[106] First, there is the lack of any effective means—in the absence of market signals—for measuring the costs of a possible allocation or distribution in lost opportunities. When prices are set by the state, without reference to demand or relative scarcities, calculations aimed at minimizing cost or maximizing effect are doomed. Prices unrelated to supply and demand mean either formal rationing or standing in line. Secondly, there is no stimulus to assimilate innovations, for example new technical equipment, for these usually reduce output in the short term, thus threatening plan fulfilment. Here too we must not overlook the inherent conservatism of economic bureaucracies, which, like all bureaucracies, value steadiness and predictability above initiative and imagination. Thirdly,

[105] *Eurocommunism and the State*, 22.

[106] For an accessible and succinct discussion, see A. Nove, *The Economics of Feasible Socialism* (London: Allen & Unwin, 1983), Pt. II. For a more balanced analysis, which considers the structural failings of market systems as well as those of centrally planned economies, see R. Nelson, 'Assessing Private Enterprise: An Exegesis of Tangled Doctrine', *The Bell Journal of Economics*, 12 (Spring 1981), 93–111.

central planning is deficient in the refinement necessary to produce a steady stream of sophisticated consumer goods, since *ex ante* decision-making, in an uncompetitive environment, cannot respond quickly to ever-shifting and developing consumer preferences. Last, but not least, in what possible terms can plan indicators be set to measure the freshness of lettuce or the beauty of a new car? The subordination of quality to quantifiable plan targets seems a permanent feature of centrally administered economies. But no amount of empirical evidence can shake the Marxist conviction that class relations under capitalism are necessarily exploitative and imply irreconcilable divisions of interest between ruling and subject classes. For Marx and Engels, as for their epigones, the inherently conflictual nature of class relations means that bourgeois gains can only come at the expense of the proletariat, regardless of any apparently contrary facts. This axiom is crucial to Marxist doctrine and supplies its *raison d'être*. For if capitalism can indeed satisfy the material interests of the whole community, then communism is a Utopian dream rather than an objective historical necessity. So—in Marxist eyes—liberal democracy, by according a 'privileged position' to business, merely confirms and enforces the exploitation of the masses. This thesis ranks alongside economic determinism as an article of blind Marxian faith, rooted in first principles and little justified by historical experience. If, however, one rejects the idea of intrinsic class conflict, there is no point in referring to the liberal state as a capitalist or bourgeois state.

But when Marxists attack liberal democracy as a sham, they are not simply referring to bogus claims to govern in the general interest. Not only does 'bourgeois' democracy fail to produce government *for* the people; it also reneges on its claim to be government *by* the people. Liberal democracy pretends faithfully to reflect the majority will, a product of the independently formulated interests and desires of the electorate. But Marxists invariably deny this claim, on the assumption that power necessarily follows property, universal suffrage notwithstanding. Some—the Eurocommunists for example—are willing to accept that liberal constitutional forms could eventually express the popular will, but not before structural reforms and trends undermine capitalism's ability to distort the electoral process through financial contributions (bribes), ownership of the mass media, and so forth. One need not, however, resort to Marxist reductionism in order to question the belief that liberal democracy merely implements some autonomous 'will of the people'. Scepticism about such claims was also voiced, roughly a century ago, by a trio of thinkers now known as the classical élitists (Gaetano Mosca, Vilfredo Pareto, Robert Michels), who contended that the universal need for expertise, along with the imperatives of large-scale organization and the inevitable apathy of the masses, meant that a manipulative élite would always rule in its own interests, whatever constitutional mechanisms were in force. Mosca, arguably the founder of this conservative school of thought, gave a famous and concise statement of the general élitist position:

Among the constant facts and tendencies that are to be found in all political organisms, one is so obvious that it is apparent to the most casual eye. In all societies—from societies that are very meagerly developed and have barely attained the dawnings of civilization, down to the most advanced and powerful societies—two classes of people appear—a class that rules and a class that is ruled. The first class, always the less numerous, performs all political functions, monopolizes power and enjoys the advantages that power brings, whereas the second, the more numerous class, is directed and controlled by the first, in a manner that is now more or less legal, now more or less arbitrary and violent.[107]

It follows that democracy is a myth, whose popular appeal is proof of man's gullibility and need to shelter behind comforting illusions. As for liberal politics, which trades on this myth, it is little more than a pretentious fraud.

Élitist arguments, however, were neither clear nor rigorous. Mosca, together with Pareto and Michels, assumed that government could never be accountable to the governed, but they were nowhere precise about the exact meaning or possible meanings of accountability in this context. How would we recognize it if we came across it? Neither did the élitists

---

[107] *The Ruling Class*, ed. A. Livingston and trans. H. D. Kahn (New York: McGraw-Hill, 1939), 50.

make any systematic attempt to gather and weigh evidence. Their method has been characterized as 'proof by anecdote'.[108] Their generalizations do not grow out of the data; rather the data are simply appended to the generalizations as examples. Despite these methodological flaws, élitist arguments were absorbed by later academic *defenders* of liberal democracy, some of whom admitted that democratic elections in the West express what 'is largely not a genuine but a manufactured will', since 'the will of the people is the product and not the motive power of the political process'.[109] As early as 1942, Joseph Schumpeter declared that this manufacturing process 'is exactly analogous to the ways of commercial advertising'. He proceeded to elaborate: 'We find the same attempts to contact the subconscious. We find the same technique of creating favorable and unfavorable associations which are the more effective the less rational they are.'[110] Slogans, half-truths, marching tunes, razzmatazz, back-room deals, deliberate distortions, bribes, rigid party discipline—these are not avoidable deviations from democratic purity. On the contrary, they 'are the essence of politics'.[111] While Schumpeter concedes that the competitive element in the parliamentary system does allow for some measure of responsible government and citizen choice, and is therefore democratic, he also urges us to recognize that voters are inevitably manipulated and do not themselves decide policies or issues. Western democracy amounts not to popular rule but to a system of *limitation* and *control* of power.

Whether or not we agree with Schumpeter's pessimistic assessment of human potential ('the electoral mass is incapable of action other than a stampede') or his contention that élite rule is unavoidable, it is hard to resist the conclusion that he is right about the constricted nature of democracy as actually practised.[112] In our highly centralized societies,

---

[108] G. Hands, 'Roberto Michels and the Study of Political Parties', *British Journal of Political Science*, 1 (Apr. 1971), 157.

[109] J. A. Schumpeter, *Capitalism, Socialism and Democracy* (New York: Harper & Row, 1950), 263. See also G. Sartori, *Democratic Theory* (Detroit: Wayne State University Press, 1962), 77.

[110] *Capitalism, Socialism and Democracy*, 263.

[111] Ibid. 283.

[112] Ibid.

where popular participation is kept to a minimum, where rational debate is replaced by slick advertising techniques, and where remote bureaucracies and multinational corporations make major decisions concerning the distribution of resources in the community, no one can afford to be sanguine about the actual degree of popular rule. The gap between liberal democratic rhetoric and empirical reality remains wide. But while Marxists are, I think, correct to point to the hypocrisy and élitism of liberal democracy, they are wrong to attribute these tendencies solely to the economic power of the possessing classes. As Max Weber, following the classical élitists, persuasively argued, bureaucratic and political organizations offer *independent* sources of power and manipulation. Anyone who doubts the validity of Weber's argument need only cast an eye on communist or former communist countries, in which there is/was little private ownership of the means of production, yet (to put it mildly) no shortage of élite domination.

IV Concluding Remarks

Marx's critique of liberal democracy (largely accepted as gospel by later Marxists) captures a part of the truth, but only a small part. Turning first to his philosophical objections, we can readily agree that bourgeois man lacks communal solidarity and that existing political arrangements, governed by the principles of self-interest and 'Thou shalt not' rather than 'love' or 'participation', both reflect and foster this deficiency—if deficiency it is. Marx was also right to underline the limitations of a concept of citizenship that restricts itself to quinquennial visits to the polling booth and completely ignores the power relations that confront people every day in their place of work, where many 'free' citizens sink to the level of obedient servants. But from these valid premises, Marx made fallacious deductions, the first being that civil society was nothing more than a realm of slavery and degradation, a lonely, miserable 'war of all against all'. In contrast to Hegel, he greatly underestimated the degree of self-expression and emotional gratification attainable through the exclusive, small-scale institutions of civil society—families, clubs, businesses, churches, trade unions, professional bodies, pressure groups—that mediate between the individual and the state. For Marx and his later disciples, such divisive forms of association were characteristic of man's 'prehistory'. Under communism, they would either disappear or transform themselves into instruments of the collective. Civil and political society would merge into a seamless whole, thus rendering obsolete the age-old distinction between particular and universal interests. The Marxist ideal rests upon an unmediated family-like community, coextensive with humanity as a whole. Yet it may be that the non-universal, group solidarity of bourgeois society is the best men and women can achieve. Can communal sentiment ever transcend localized boundaries to encompass the entire human race? And even if it can, is all-inclusive communitarianism the best or only way to satisfy our distinctive human potential?

In his contempt for the particularity and selfishness of bourgeois life, Marx was also moved to denigrate individual human rights as well as the negative freedoms they were designed to guarantee. Again, we see that he refused to assign intrinsic value to the diversity and plurality of modern society, since certain accepted practices and forms of expression were antithetical to the type of tightly integrated community he envisaged, one which would obliterate the (to his mind) artificial, corrupt barrier between 'public' and 'private'. He wanted social being to encompass all the dimensions of individual existence. Morally, and indeed ontologically, he asserted the priority of the 'whole' over the individual parts. Starting from the premiss that the individual is nothing outside society, which alone confers human substance, Marx apparently arrived at the conclusion that society is everything, the sole reference-point before which conduct is judged and justified. This, at any rate, is how most observers have interpreted his call for the total socialization of individual life. Had he witnessed the terrible events of this century, he might have learned to appreciate how the bourgeois values of independence and privacy uphold the integrity of the human personality against the depredations of an all-powerful state. He might also have developed misgivings about his belief that the purpose of politics is to mould human beings after an abstract pattern, as if they were, like a potter's clay, more or less worthless in their present condition. A paradox emerges here: the attempt to reconstruct man as an integral being threatens the very human dignity it is meant to restore. Where liberal democracy scores heavily is in its recognition of such paradoxes. As a form of governance, it eschews moral perfectionism and takes heed of Machiavelli's warning: 'Men commit the error of not knowing when to limit their hopes.'

Marx's sociological critique of liberal democracy perhaps has more to commend it. The thesis that our political and juridical institutions systematically and exclusively serve the interests of the dominant economic classes has a surface plausibility. What Lindblom labels 'the privileged position of business' is fairly transparent, and the panoply of law sustains a distribution of property that is grossly unequal. It is also undeniable that most ordinary folk view the political world as remote and unapproachable, beyond their influence or comprehension—a sphere reserved for their 'social betters'. 'Government *by* the people' seems a hollow slogan, even to many who support the existing system. But Marx's analysis falls down in two respects. First, it is by no means obvious that the 'privileged position of business' operates to the detriment of the workers. Marx (in common with all Marxists) sees capitalism as a zero-sum game where the capitalists cannot be winners unless the workers are losers. As we have seen, there are good reasons for questioning this assumption. By protecting capitalism, the liberal state is probably maximizing the material living standards of the great bulk of the population.

My second, and more fundamental, objection to Marx's sociological critique of liberal democracy strikes at the heart of historical materialism. In his effort to penetrate beneath the 'appearances' of society and history, Marx reduced complex realities to a single organizing principle: the causal primacy of economics, Marxism's 'hidden God', as Croce aptly described it.[113] Like any other metaphysical system, Marxism tends to turn a deaf ear to the voice of fact, thus forcing events or

[113] B. Croce, *Storia della storiografia italiana nel secolo decimonono*, ii (Bari: Laterza, 1964), 125.

persons into prefabricated moulds. Hence the assumption that political power flows solely from economic power. While many Marxists, and Marx himself, admit that the state can, in certain circumstances at least, function in accordance with its own logic, they invariably shrink from the full consequences of this admission. Gestures towards the 'relative autonomy' of the state must always be followed by a resounding 'but' which adds the Marxist icing to an otherwise unremarkable cake: 'in the final analysis', 'in the last instance', 'at the end of the day', state power is class power, itself determined by the underlying exigencies of capital. For to concede that political or bureaucratic position constitutes an *independent* source of power, free of class control, is to enter the alien and forbidden land of Weberian theory. It is to abandon Marxist analysis altogether.

Kolakowski has written that liberal democracy 'carries a great number of vices and only one virtue'. 'All its blemishes and dangers', he continues, 'are easily found in the Marxist literature. And its only virtue is that nobody as yet has invented anything better.'[114] Is he right about this virtue? Our remaining task is to examine what Marxists would put in place of Western democracy. As we shall see, the weaknesses in their analysis of existing forms seriously flaw their vision of the future.

[114] 'The Myth of Human Self-identity', in *The Socialist Idea*, 34.

3 Marxist Democracy?

I Preliminary Remarks

WHILE Marxists tirelessly decry the hypocrisy and deficiencies of 'bourgeois' democracy, they have expended much less ink and energy on the development of a feasible alternative. To some degree, this limitation is a matter of principle. Marxists, in separating their own position from that of 'Utopian' socialists, have always refrained from presenting a detailed and comprehensive plan of the future society. Such reticence owes much to the inescapable logic of economic determinism. If the mode of political life essentially reflects the material conditions of existence, then the classic political problems of power and authority are of secondary importance. Why devote attention to surface phenomena which only rarely affect the underlying reality? If, for example, economic oppression is the ultimate source of all oppression, the imminent elimination of the former obviates the need for an extended analysis of the latter. And to those who view economic liberation as liberation *tout court*, traditional questions about the specifically political expression of human freedom are more or less irrelevant. Small wonder that Marxists, when speculating on the perfect social order, rarely get beyond woolly platitudes. Where we might expect to find coherent theory, we encounter little more than rhetoric about 'the people controlling their own destiny', or 'the self-government of the producers'. In order, therefore, to set out what Marxists would put in place of so-called bourgeois democracy, we are necessarily obliged to impose system and order on scattered remarks and observations that are often half-baked or polemical. What we discover is that the Marxist tradition offers no single alternative to the practices and institutions of liberal politics. 'Democracy', literally translated from the ancient Greek, means 'power of the people'. In Marxist discourse, we can discern three distinct—indeed contradictory—concepts of how this power should be manifested. For the sake of simplicity, these can be labelled the participatory, the parliamentary, and the vanguard models of democracy. Why this diversity in Marxist projections of the future? In what follows, I shall argue that each of the afore-mentioned models is irreconcilable with one or more basic features of the Marxist *weltanschauung*. There would appear to be no conceivable theory of democracy that could accom-modate *all* of the doctrine's conflicting desiderata. Hence, different Marxists will adopt different conceptions, depending on the weight they attach to different Marxist values.

II The Participatory Model

It is symptomatic of the dearth of Marxist political thought that Marx's own most substantial reflections on socialist democracy were set down when he was only 25 years old, and never revised or seriously developed thereafter. Even these reflections, which form part of his *Critique of Hegel's Philo-sophy of the State*, are incomplete and obscure. Yet Marx, in this early manuscript, formulated certain principles that have influenced subsequent Marxist thinking.

His observations on democracy make up an essential in-gredient of his theoretical response to the modern dichotomy between civil society and political life, between *homme* and *citoyen*. As already detailed in Chapter 2, Marx denounces bourgeois civil society, based on unrestrained individualism, as a violation of man's social being. Individualism in this sense implies a model of man as an entity whose social relations are nothing more than a means to his own private ends; it sees individual existence as man's supreme purpose and juxtaposes the larger community to the individual person as something external and distant. Within this context, the liberal political constitution offers but an illusion of common identity and purpose; it (the constitution) becomes a kind of *'religion* of the people's life', 'the affirmation of their own alienation', 'the heaven of their universality in contrast to the

particular *mundane existence* of their actuality'.[1] What liberal
constitutionalism provides is *political* emancipation, where
the citizen, separated from his concrete 'actuality', is endowed
with a delusive 'abstract' freedom. What the liberal state cannot supply is *human* emancipation, the realization of man as
a 'species-being', 'the unity of man with man', a condition
where citizenship, now formal and meaningless, would become an internalized social force. Marx thus struggled to
create in his imagination a society that would overcome the
horrors of social atomization, that would produce integrated
human beings. He referred to this noble vision as 'true
democracy'.

Although he does not mention the word communism in his
Critique of Hegel, 'what Marx terms "democracy" is not
fundamentally different from what he will later call "communism"'.[2] True democracy would abolish the alienation
between the individual and the political community by resolv-
ing the split between the 'egoistic' interests of individuals in
civil society and the social character of political life. What is
at present only ideal (universal political participation) must
become actual: 'In democracy the *formal* principle is at the
same time the *material* principle.'[3] According to Marx, ex-
tending the franchise to the masses is the way to unify the
ideal and the real. Using convoluted language of Hegelian
provenance, he describes how the attainment of universal
suffrage would be a revolutionary act, transcending the division
between state and civil society:

Only in *unlimited voting*, active as well as passive, does civil society
actually rise to an abstraction of itself, to *political* existence as its
true universal and essential existence. But the realization of this
abstraction is also the transcendence of the abstraction. By making
its *political existence* actual as its *true* existence, civil society also
makes its civil existence *unessential* in contrast to its political existence. And with the one thing separated, the other, its opposite, falls.

[1] *Critique of Hegel's Philosophy of the State*, in *Writings of the Young
Marx on Philosophy and Society*, trans. and ed. L. D. Easton and K. H.
Guddat (New York: Doubleday, 1967), 176.
[2] S. Avineri, *The Social and Political Thought of Karl Marx* (Cambridge:
Cambridge University Press, 1968), 34. R. N. Hunt makes the same point in
The Political Ideas of Marx and Engels, i (London: Macmillan, 1975), 75.
[3] *Writings of the Young Marx*, 174.

Within the *abstract political state* the reform of voting is the *dissolution* of the state, but likewise, the *dissolution of civil society*.[4]

Loosely translated, this passage indicates that both civil society and the state would be swept away in their old forms and superseded by a higher unity where neither would be distinct from the other. The chief characteristic of the old order, egoism, would disappear in favour of species-life. This transformation would be achieved, in the case of civil society, by 'making its *political existence* actual'; that is, by turning private property into common property. Man's social essence as a communal being, which had been stolen from him and transferred to the 'heavenly' sphere of bourgeois politics, would now become actuated in his 'mundane existence'. Civil society as a differentiated arena of private interest would therefore vanish. In the political realm, class or rank would no longer stand between the person and the universality of the body politic. The act of the state in granting universal suffrage, Marx concludes, will be its last act as a state. For once its universal nature is fulfilled, once politics is introduced into the everyday, productive life of each and every citizen, the state becomes redundant as a separate organization standing over the people. But as Hunt reminds us:

To say that the old state would 'dissolve' is not to say that the polity itself would dissolve, that there would be no arrangements at all for making and carrying out collective decisions. The authentic functions of the old state would be *aufgehoben* [Marx's term], preserved in a higher form. Marx did not want to call these functions 'political,' or to call the new polity a 'state,' since both these words smacked of the despised present.[5]

Public business would still be attended to, but it would be the activity of ordinary citizens, one activity among many they would pursue. To be more specific, 'political' deliberation and administration would be the work of everyone, on a part-time or short-term basis; it would not be sufficient to have only a *chance* to serve. The chance of every Catholic to become a priest, Marx remarked, does not produce the priesthood of all

[4] Ibid. 202.
[5] *The Political Ideas of Marx and Engels*, i, 80.

believers.[6] What makes democracy 'true' is not the equal opportunity of every citizen to devote himself to public life as something special, but the 'immediate participation of *all* in deliberating and deciding' on political matters.[7] There should be no professional bureaucrats, no professional politicians, no professional police, etc. This, and not the abolition of public business as such, is what Engels had in mind when he described the 'withering away of the state' under communism:

The society that will organize production on the basis of a free and equal association of the producers will put the whole machinery of the state where it will then belong: into the museum of antiquities, by the side of the spinning wheel and the bronze ax.[8]

To the modern observer, Marx's ascription of revolutionary transformative powers to universal suffrage seems bizarre. Yet we must remember that he was writing in 1843, when 'one person, one vote' was nowhere more than a cherished hope. Whatever the merits of his youthful optimism about the effects of popular sovereignty, it is necessary to clarify what Marx meant by 'the immediate participation of all'—a resonant but ambiguous phrase. On his definition, true democracy was 'the self-determination of the people',[9] but what exact form would this take? The answer is hardly obvious. As already mentioned, Marx wanted (literally) every adult to partake in tasks now executed by full-time functionaries and politicians—'stateparasites', as he was later to describe them. In some respects, his political theory falls within that tradition which associates the representative principle with a withdrawal from social engagement. Rousseau, writing a century before Marx, is here typical:

Sovereignty . . . cannot be represented; it lies essentially in the general will. . . . Every law the people has not ratified in person is null and void. . . . The people of England regards itself as free; but it is grossly mistaken; it is free only during the election of members of

6 *Writings of the Young Marx*, 190.
7 Ibid. 196.
8 *The Origin of the Family, Private Property and the State*, in *Marx & Engels: Basic Writings on Politics and Philosophy*, ed. L. S. Feuer (New York: Doubleday, 1959), 394.
9 *Writings of the Young Marx*, 175.

parliament. As soon as they are elected, slavery overtakes it, and it is nothing.[10]

Rousseau's hostility to representative government stems from his image of an ideal society in which the public/private distinction is but a grim memory, because politics is totally integrated with daily life. For Marx as well, participation confined to the periodic election of deputies 'is precisely the *expression* of the separation and merely dualistic unity' between the civil and political spheres.[11] Such limited participation, in other words, is a ritualistic affirmation of man's alienation from the bourgeois state. Marx also sides with Rousseau against the liberal position that it is simply quantities of self-seeking individuals that comprise the ideal polity —individuals pursuing their own narrow interests and electing deputies to represent these interests. Marx counters this individualistic concept by arguing that the polity is (or should be) made up of individuals acting on common principles and renouncing their purely selfish interests: 'Not all as individuals, but the individuals as all.'[12] True universality, like Rousseau's general will, can emerge only when individual citizens hold the common good uppermost in their minds, when they behave as species-beings and not as self-centred monads. One must not confuse the public interest with the sum total of private interests.

In Marx's opinion, then, the classic representative principle, as defined by the liberal tradition, fails to achieve its two main goals: (i) accountability, and (ii) protection of the public interest. Nevertheless, Rousseau's contempt for representation *per se* was not shared by Marx. Ever anxious to offer a practical alternative, he accepted the necessity of a certain amount of delegation in modern society. For, at any given time, it would be impossible for 'all' to decide upon and execute the laws of the land. Here we must focus upon his intriguing, if ill-explained, distinction between 'active' and 'passive' voting.[13] According to Hunt, Marx expected that the people would vote

[10] J.-J. Rousseau, *The Social Contract and Discourses*, trans. and ed. G. D. H. Cole (London: Dent, 1913), 78.
[11] *Writings of the Young Marx*, 200.
[12] Ibid. 197.
[13] Ibid. 202.

on important issues directly, either by referendum or at specially convened mass meetings. This, to be sure, is the most plausible meaning that can be attached to 'active' suffrage. As for 'passive' voting, this presumably meant (we cannot be sure) electing deputies who would attend to matters of legislative detail as well as administer existing laws.[14] Decades later, when commenting favourably on the Paris Commune of 1871, Marx added some details to his earlier, lamentably sketchy description of socialist democracy. He first of all endorsed the communard belief that deputies should see themselves as mandated delegates, or 'communal agents', subject to recall and revocation at short notice. Close popular control would prevent all functionaries, not excluding judges, from raising themselves above 'real society'; and remuneration restricted to 'workmen's wages' would discourage place-seeking for motives of personal gain. Marx also pointed out, with approbation, that the Commune assembly was (in conception at any rate) 'a working, not a parliamentary body, executive and legislative at the same time'.[15] On this view, executive functions were no longer 'the hidden attributes of a trained caste', but tasks which could be publicly and effectively undertaken by any workman acting in his role as a deputy under public supervision.[16] Marx was convinced that the growth of the state bureaucracy into a 'huge governmental parasite, entoiling the social body like a boa constrictor', was encouraged, if not wholly explained, by the formal separation of legislative and executive functions.[17] Unless socialist democracy eliminated this separation, the 'whole sham of state-mysteries and statepretensions' could rise again to haunt it.[18]

In his 1891 Introduction to *The Civil War in France*, Engels identified the Commune with 'the dictatorship of the proletariat'.[19] This remark is puzzling, as the dictatorship is, in Marxist literature, a *transitional* phase before full-blown communism, whereas the Commune, as depicted by Marx,

[14] *The Political Ideas of Marx and Engels*, i, 81–2.
[15] K. Marx, *The Civil War in France* (Peking: Foreign Languages Press, 1970), 232–3.
[16] Ibid. 170.
[17] Ibid. 228.
[18] Ibid. 170.
[19] Ibid. 18.

apparently resembles the final, 'stateless' form of 'the self-determination of the people'. Read in context, Engels's words seem designed to reassure social-democratic 'philistines' (his term) who trembled at the thought of dictatorship. In any case, it is perhaps misleading to place so much emphasis on Marx's rather meagre analysis of the Paris rebellion. In private he expressed misgivings about the durability of the new communal order, and his doubts were confirmed by its bloody suppression just two months after its inception. What is more, the communards, who showed not the slightest interest in 'scientific socialism', mainly belonged to radical groupings (Blanquists, Proudhonists) that Marx had vilified.[20] Norberto Bobbio is not altogether wrong when he argues that 'Marx had no intention of issuing prescriptions for the future through these few formulations', and that only 'by abusing authority have the five or six theses been transformed into a treatise on public law'.[21] On the other hand, Marx did describe the Commune as *the political form of social emancipation, of the liberation of labour from the usurpations ... of the monopolists of the means of labour*.[22] Taken in conjunction with the 1843 *Critique*, his observations on the Commune help us to make sense of the famous, but maddeningly abstract, last paragraph of the 'Jewish Question':

Only when the actual, individual man has taken back into himself the abstract citizen and in his everyday life, his individual work, and his individual relationships has become a *species-being*, only when he has recognized and organized his own powers as *social* powers so that social force is no longer separated from him as *political* power, only then is human emancipation complete.[23]

Stated otherwise, socialist men and women would no longer separate their own collective power from themselves and surrender it, as alienated political power, to the trained caste of 'stateparasites'[24] who run the existing polity. Moreover, their own activities as citizens would cease to be sporadic and

[20] M. Levin, *Marx, Engels and Liberal Democracy* (London: Macmillan, 1989), 113–18.
[21] 'Is there a Marxist Theory of the State?', *Telos*, 35 (Spring 1978), 16.
[22] *The Civil War in France*, 171.
[23] *Writings of the Young Marx*, 241.
[24] *The Civil War in France*, 169.

unreal, instead becoming an essential part of their daily lives: they would thus absorb 'the abstract citizen' back into themselves. As Hunt accurately remarks, 'Marx embraced communism to resolve the political as much as the socioeconomic dilemmas of modern society'.[25]

Hunt finds the source of Marx's ideal polity in ancient Greece. It is indeed reasonable to suppose that Marx shared with most of his educated contemporaries in Germany an exaggerated admiration of classical antiquity, especially Athens in the Age of Pericles (mid-fifth century BC). And his ideal *is* very close to Periclean Athens, if Pericles' famous funeral oration, as reported by Thucydides, is a reliable guide to the workings of that distant civilization.[26] Important matters, both legislative and executive, were resolved by the entire citizenry, exercising its sovereignty in frequent assemblies. More mundane business was delegated to the Council of Five Hundred, selected annually by lot from among candidates elected in the several districts of the city-state. All other officials (tax collectors, generals, etc.) were likewise selected each year by lot or by election. There was no permanent, professional civil service, save for a few lower-level functionaries. As for judicial tasks, these were dealt with entirely by huge juries, chosen in the same manner as the Council. Apathy was frowned upon and civic competence was assumed to be a requirement of citizenship.

The question, of course, is whether a model appropriate to ancient and simpler times could possibly have any relevance to modern technological society. As a nation, ancient Athens was small, in both population and physical size. Furthermore, it depended upon slaves to perform routine productive labour, thus giving citizens the leisure to engage in communal activities and deliberations. Still, many Marxists have concluded that the participatory model is the only form of governance that can cater for 'the self-determination of the people', Marxism's Holy Grail. Even Lenin, in one of his rare idealistic moods, gave his emphatic approval to Marx's participatory

---

[25] *The Political Ideas of Marx and Engels*, i, 82.
[26] Thucydides, *The Peloponnesian War*, trans. and ed. R. Warner (Baltimore: Penguin, 1954), 115–23.

prescriptions. In *The State and Revolution*, a much-read work written just before the October revolution, he aspired to 'the most complete democracy', where 'parliamentarism', understood 'as the division of labour between the legislative and the executive, as a privileged position for the deputies', would be consigned to the dustbin of history.[27] Three aspects of Lenin's Utopia require stress. First, all state officials, including deputies, would be 'elected and subject to recall *at any time*, their salaries reduced to the level of ordinary "workmen's wages"'.[28] They would be mere delegates carrying out explicit instructions—humble servants of the people in the truest sense. Secondly, representative institutions would be converted from 'talking shops into "working" bodies' that would not only pass laws but execute them as well.[29] Thirdly, the mass of the population would, at one time or another, take part in the quotidian administration of the state. Indeed, '*everybody*, without exception', would 'perform "state functions"', since these functions 'have become so simplified and can be reduced to such exceedingly simple operations of registration, filing and checking that they can be easily performed by every literate person'.[30] The point for Lenin—as it was for Marx, whose ideas the Russian merely reproduced—was to break down the artificial barriers between rulers and ruled, so that '*all* will govern in turn and will soon become accustomed to no one governing'.[31]

The notion that the 'pigsty'[32] of parliamentary democracy must be smashed and replaced by representative organs of a soviet- or commune-type received some practical expression in the early days of the Russian Revolution, when spontaneous forms of popular democracy sprouted up to challenge the old and rapidly disintegrating order. After the unceremonious collapse of the Tsarist state, a brief experiment in liberal constitutionalism was overwhelmed by the grassroots revolutionary upsurge. While the emergent council structure owed its exis-

---

[27] V. I. Lenin, *The State and Revolution* (Moscow: Progress Publishers, 1949), 19, 45.
[28] Ibid. 41.
[29] Ibid. 43.
[30] Ibid. 107, 41.
[31] Ibid. 106.
[32] Ibid. 43.

tence to nothing but the organizational impulses of the people themselves, the Bolsheviks seized control with the slogan, 'All power to the soviets'. But, ironically, it was Lenin himself who decided to destroy the autonomy of these local organs of self-government. For him, a new system of proletarian democracy was all very well in principle, but in practice it was first necessary to deal with 'the workers who have been thoroughly corrupted by capitalism',[33] not excepting those who were ostensibly revolutionary but nevertheless hostile to Bolshevism, that is, populists and Mensheviks. The concentration of power in the hands of the Party proceeded apace during the years following the revolution. In 1919 the Party Congress officially proclaimed the goal of obtaining complete control of all worker organizations. The soviets, through force of arms where necessary, were to become mere executive organs of revolutionary activity, transmitting and implementing the decisions of the Bolshevik élite.[34]

Lenin's apparent hypocrisy incurred the wrath of a group of thinkers known as 'council communists', the most prominent of whom was Anton Pannekoek, a Dutch professor of astronomy, no less. According to him, the Bolsheviks were confusing the dictatorship *of* the proletariat with the dictatorship *over* the proletariat. Socialism was not simply a matter of public property or nationalization. Effective power must be placed directly in the hands of the people, for as Karl Korsch, another council communist, put it:

the single productive class of active workers will not as such be freer, their ways of life and labour will not be more worthy of a human being, through replacing the bosses installed by the owners of private capital by officials installed by the state government.

Instead, socialists should strive for what he called 'industrial democracy', the 'direct control and administration of every

[33] Ibid. 93.

[34] Still, the policy of subordinating the soviets to a single will was not entirely successful until the 1930s, when Stalin's Terror held full sway. According to a Party report on the 1926 elections, for example, 'hostile class elements' had managed to influence the campaign and penetrate the soviets. In tones of horror, the report mentioned cases in which certain rural soviets actually had the temerity to pass anti-communist resolutions. See B. Moore, *Soviet Politics: The Dilemma of Power* (Cambridge, Mass.: Harvard University Press, 1950), 128–38.

branch of industry...by the community of participating workers, and through organs determined by themselves'.[35]

Antonio Gramsci, though a loyal admirer of Lenin, briefly found himself in sympathy with the council communists. Like them, he was excited by the spontaneous self-organization of the Russian proletariat; unlike them, however, he eventually (and no doubt regretfully) came to accept that Lenin's demotion of the soviets was both necessary and proper. During Italy's *biennio rosso* of 1919–20, a period of heightened industrial militancy and civil unrest, the Sardinian revolutionary was the main inspiration behind the factory council movement in Italy. In a succession of articles and editorials for the newspaper *Ordine Nuovo*, he produced what remains to this day the most detailed and interesting of Marxist proposals for industrial democracy. His subsequent change of heart tells us much about the contradictory nature of Marxism. Let me elaborate.

Marx himself, in keeping with his studied vagueness about the communist ideal, had little or nothing to say about the mechanisms of worker participation at the point of production. Indeed, before the First World War Marxists tended to avoid the subject altogether, as it was closely associated with Proudhon (the 'father' of anarchism) and, later, with the anarcho-syndicalists (who wanted to base the new society on the trade union movement). Even after the Russian experience appeared to prove that state-appointed bosses were no less oppressive than capitalist bosses, there remained a widespread feeling that, *pace* the council communists, worker self-management was not a fit topic for a Marxist to explore. For the youthful editor of *Ordine Nuovo*, on the other hand, the centrality of production in the Marxist view of history meant that socialist democracy should be firmly rooted 'in the murky depths of the factory' and 'generated by the associative experience of the proletarian class'.[36] The division between man as a private person and man as an abstract citizen will be overcome only when the workers *directly* control the social condi-

[35] *Karl Korsch: Revolutionary Theory*, ed. D. Kellner (Austin: University of Texas Press, 1977), 18–22.

[36] *Selections from Political Writings: 1910–1920*, ed. Q. Hoare and trans. J. Mathews (London: Lawrence and Wishart, 1977), 261, 76.

tions of their labour and material existence. Only then will citizenship, now an abstraction, remote from daily life, become 'actual', a function of one's status as a producer. Though reminiscent of syndicalist variants of anarchism, Gramsci's council theory was impeccably Marxist in its assumption that 'man' expresses himself in his labour, by progressively transforming nature to suit his ever-expanding needs. It follows that all political, social, and cultural life must emerge organically (so to speak) from productive activity, which is somehow more 'real' than other types of activity.

In the proletarian democracy envisaged by Gramsci, the factory council would act as the basic unit of governmental and industrial organization. Unlike membership of a political party or trade union, participation in the factory council would not be voluntary. One would not 'join' a council in the same way one decides to become a member of a voluntary association. *All* workers, even managers and administrators, would automatically be part of the council system by virtue of being producers, and all would be eligible to vote for the delegates who would represent them in their respective councils.[37] Gramsci noted that factories are divided, for technical reasons, into workshops or separate production units. Representation would be founded upon these units, the boundaries of which would be determined functionally by the products they supplied. Significantly, modern shop organization usually includes workers of different skills and trades, brought together for a common purpose. As part of his campaign for councils, Gramsci attacked the way trade unions combine workers 'on the basis of the tools they use or the material they transform', thus fixing workers in their particular capacities and attitudes and discouraging them from experiencing 'the unity of the industrial process'.[38] Unions are *exclusive*; councils are *inclusive*. In his denigration of the former, Gramsci differed sharply from the syndicalists.

The principle of representation corresponding to units of production, already enshrined at the plant level, would also characterize workers' democracy as a whole: individual fac-

---

[37] Ibid. 295, 101.
[38] Ibid. 110.

tory councils would be linked together through ward councils, regional councils, and so on. The delegates in these 'higher' bodies would be indirectly elected: for example, the factory council would select one of its members to sit on the ward council, which would in turn nominate a member or members to represent it in the municipal council, etc. In this new order, interests would be aggregated on production, rather than strict territorial, lines. For, according to Gramsci, political representation must reflect 'the functions of labour and the order that the working class adopts naturally in the process of skilled industrial production'. But, contrary to appearances, he did not intend to restrict representation to factory workers. Farm labourers, he hinted, would have councils of their own; and the ward council, we are told in a brief aside, should somehow seek to 'incorporate delegates' from among the service workers (waiters, tram-drivers, railwaymen, road-sweepers) living in the ward. Yet he also claimed that 'factory delegates are the sole and authentic... representatives of the proletarian class by virtue of their being elected at the workplace'. Service workers (perhaps because they were not 'productive') seem to have been an afterthought.[39] We should not, however, be unduly troubled by such gaps or inconsistencies in the theory. *Ordine Nuovo* devoted only a few vague passages to the mechanisms and procedures of proletarian democracy at the higher levels. Attention was concentrated, instead, on the tasks of the factory council.

While Gramsci had no intention of eliminating authority in plant-level industrial relations, such authority would be responsive to the wishes of the labour force. The factory council would assume the internal functions of planning, co-ordinating, and disciplining previously performed by the capitalist(s).[40] The council would allocate resources within the factory, set production schedules, estimate labour needs, hire and fire, organize the work process, and 'instil a conscious and voluntary discipline', based on 'a producer's mentality— the mentality of a creator of history'.[41] Voluntary discipline would not negate the need for hierarchy within the plant.

[39] Ibid. 66–7, 91, 116–17.
[40] Ibid. 77.
[41] Ibid. 101.

Day-to-day supervisory functions would have to be performed by professional managers and skilled technicians, but they would derive their authority from the council, the ultimate source of authoritative decisions. Just as democratic procedures would determine what goes on in an individual factory, so too would they determine the productive activities undertaken in the wider society. The free market would be replaced by a system of 'horizontal and vertical planning'.[42] On this model, what is produced, earmarked for consumption, and set aside for investment is decided not by a competitive price mechanism but by a centralized, accountable network of producers' councils. Economic decisions, in other words, are arrived at through a political process that reflects the preferences of producers, as distinct from those of consumers. If the model were implemented, information concerning plant capacity and labour and investment requirements would, one presumes, be supplied in plan proposals formulated by lower units of production and then presented for approval or (much more likely) modification to higher-level councils.

Modern advocates of self-management may be surprised to discover that Gramsci bore no ill will towards the technical division of labour, its narrow specialization and mindless repetition notwithstanding. On the contrary, he regarded such division as a source of solidarity and communist consciousness:

The more the proletarian specializes in a professional task, the more he feels the indispensability of his fellows, the more he experiences himself as a cell in a structured body, a body internally unified and cohesive.[43]

Gramsci had no real interest in humanizing the productive system through job rotation or any other scheme that might sacrifice technical efficiency for the sake of spontaneity or creative enrichment. In common with almost all classical Marxists, he accepted the validity of 'bourgeois systems of production and work processes', and argued that communist equality would be won 'only through an intensive productive

---

[42] Ibid. 77.
[43] L'Ordine Nuovo: 1919–1920 (Turin: Einaudi, 1954), 325: a comprehensive collection of Gramsci's articles and editorials during the years in question.

effort', not through 'disorder in production and a relaxation of work discipline'.[44] Indeed, his ideal future is one where 'the whole world' is patterned on 'a single immense factory, organised with the same precision, the same method, the same order'. In this vision, 'the order, the precision, the method that animate the factory' will be 'projected into the system of relations that ties one factory to another, one city to another, one nation to another'.[45] The 'whole world' will become an 'organic whole, a homogeneous and compact system'.[46]

Contemplating this regimented world order, where everyone would be a small cog in an unimaginably vast productive machine, we can understand why Marx—history's most renowned champion of economic planning—evaded the issue of worker control at the point of production. The plain truth is that it conflicts with central regulation of trade and industry at the national level, never mind the global level. Either Gramsci did not recognize the contradiction or he assumed it would be resolved by the general acquisition of 'communist consciousness', which would enable workers 'to comprehend what a great step forward the communist economy represents over the capitalist'.[47] Now, in some fantasy world, brimming over with collective solidarity and blessed by unity of purpose, the spontaneous preferences of individual groups of workers might automatically harmonize with the needs of the economy, as determined by the community as a whole. But surely the operative term here is 'fantasy world'. How, without presupposing a socialist version of Adam Smith's 'invisible hand', can the autonomy of the part be squared with the perfect rationality of the whole? The essence of central control of a non-market economy consists in a planning organ which conveys all necessary information to the subordinate units in the form of mandatory directives, whereby it deprives these units of independent decision-making. Even if the plan is the outcome of democratic deliberation, once formulated it must be binding on all productive enterprises. The more participation (and autonomy) on the shop-floor, the less pre-

[44] *Selections from Political Writings: 1910–1920*, 121.
[45] *L'Ordine Nuovo: 1919–1920*, 325–6.
[46] *Selections from Political Writings: 1910–1920*, 100.
[47] Ibid.

dictable the economic performance, for obvious reasons. In the interests of accurate forecasting, and the avoidance of waste which is the inevitable result of getting a forecast wrong, the holistically administered economy would be tempted to limit or even discard self-management. Lenin, for his part, refused to shrink from these consequences, ridiculing the idea of industrial democracy as 'half-baked and theoretically false'.[48] Marx himself was never so forthright, but, unless I err, one can find in his writings not a single passage where he unambiguously favours the kind of worker participation demanded by some of his later disciples. At one point, he does write:

If co-operative production ... is to supersede the capitalist system, if united co-operative societies are to regulate national production upon a common plan, thus ... putting an end to the constant anarchy and periodical convulsions which are the fatality of capitalist production ... what else, gentlemen, would it be but Communism, 'possible' Communism?[49]

But this could simply mean that the 'co-operative societies' (and Marx never describes them) make sure that local units efficiently fulfil the obligatory targets specified by the 'common plan', thereby avoiding 'anarchy and periodical convulsions'. Neither the quotation nor its surrounding context tells us anything about the appropriate division of power between centre and periphery. By 1921, even Gramsci, always under Lenin's spell, had abandoned his factory council theory, almost as if it were an embarrassing juvenile aberration. Making peace with Amadeo Bordiga, hitherto the fiercest critic of the theory, Gramsci concluded that central direction of the revolutionary process, via the vanguard party, should take precedence over worker autonomy. During the next few years, he paid some lip-service to the importance of councils, albeit in a subordinate role (like the Russian soviets). He was never explicit about why he chose, à la Lenin, to relegate councils. Whether he was influenced by the problems outlined here or by more immediate strategic/tactical concerns is open to

[48] V. I. Lenin, 'On Trade Unions', in *Collected Works*, xxxii (Moscow: Progress Publishers, 1960–70), 26–7.
[49] *The Civil War in France*, 73.

speculation. Gramsci was a practical politician as well as a theorist. What we can say for certain is that nowhere in his voluminous *Prison Notebooks* (composed in the 1930s) did he discuss factory councils.[50] The reader can draw his/her own conclusions.

For Marxist advocates of participatory democracy, there would appear to be two possible options. Those who wish to base the new order on workplace self-management must accept substantial market regulation of the economy, as market relations obviously allow individual productive units to exercise a considerable measure of autonomy. Although market discipline imposes constraints, these would be no greater than those suffered by capitalists in the present system. But Marxists who seek to combine participation with comprehensive planning must acknowledge that worker control within the productive unit can only be marginal. Decisions about inputs, outputs, prices, and wages will, of necessity, be made at a higher level. The main focus of participation would therefore have to be the local commune, defined in geographical terms. Let us now examine these two options.

The first—acceptance of market regulation within a framework of public ownership—was adopted by the communist regime in (now defunct) Yugoslavia. Whether the Yugoslav experiment can properly be called Marxist is a moot point, however. Marx's own implacable opposition to the market is well known and scarcely requires documentation. In his opinion, the market system and 'commodity fetishism' were inextricably linked. The market and its corollary, commodity production, weave a mystical veil that shrouds social reality, personifying objects and reifying human beings. Commodities acquire an independent status, standing opposed to labour as alien powers, mysterious, hypnotic entities, neither controlled nor consumed by those who make them. Social rela-

---

[50] For a detailed analysis of how and why Gramsci changed his mind on the subject of councils, see J. V. Femia, *Gramsci's Political Thought* (Oxford: Clarendon Press, 1981), 139–51. For a lengthy and scholarly study of Gramsci's council theory, one that pays particular attention to the theory's critics and intellectual antecedents, see D. Schecter, *Gramsci and the Theory of Industrial Democracy* (Aldershot: Gower, 1991).

tions themselves appear as relations among commodities or things, alienating people from each other, transforming human relations into purely functional or contractual ones. The market, then, is antagonistic to community life: it produces a world of isolated and egoistic individuals, bound together by calculation, by dollars and cents. Mandel follows Marx when he declares that the commodity economy leads to the '*universal* "mercenariness" of life' and encourages 'the egoist mentality of the "old Adam"'.[51] This moral and philosophical denunciation of the market system is coupled with a specifically economic critique. Because the market cuts the tie between production and consumption, 'anarchy reigns' within capitalism. It is impossible to estimate the demand for any given commodity, which means that the system suffers from an endemic tendency towards crises of overproduction. The market, a blind and irrational force, a 'master demon', must be replaced by 'social regulation of production upon a definite plan'.[52] When commodity production is finally abolished, the economy submits to 'the associated producers, rationally regulating their interchange with Nature, bringing it under their common control'.[53] For Marx (and later Marxists), doing away with market relations was the *sine qua non* of authentic socialism—a socialism combining collective solidarity, individual fulfilment, and economic abundance.

On the evidence adduced, retention of the market would not seem to be a long-term option for any Marxist worthy of the name. Yet, as we have seen, market regulation is an essential precondition for worker self-management. Hopes for a participatory form of Marxian socialism must therefore rest, primarily, with the local commune, based on a geographical area. Devolution of power would enable the citizens of the commune to exercise direct control over affairs of specific local concern. On grander issues, such as the national economic plan, citizens could participate indirectly, through their

---

[51] E. Mandel, *Marxist Economic Theory*, ii (New York: Monthly Review Press, 1968), 655.

[52] F. Engels, *Socialism: Utopian and Scientific*, in *Marx & Engels: Basic Writings*, 96, 105.

[53] K. Marx, *Capital*, iii (Moscow: Foreign Languages Publishing House, 1959), 800.

mandated delegates. In principle, these delegates could be elected by workplace, rather than territorial, constituencies. But the rationale for doing so would seem to be weakened once the fiction of worker control is jettisoned. If the plant is not itself democratically organized, why assume, as did Gramsci in his *Ordine Nuovo* days, that it is the natural basis of democratic organization in the wider community? Marx himself, perhaps because he regarded the workplace as the 'realm of necessity', governed by technical imperatives, apparently wanted democratic activities to be based on territorial, as opposed to production, units. This approach has the merit of avoiding the productivist bias of the *Ordine Nuovo* model. What about students, old-age pensioners, housewives, the chronically ill and disabled? As such people are not producers in any obvious sense, they would seem to be disenfranchised by any system of democracy that effectively restricts its sphere of operation to the workplace. In addition, it is bizarre to suppose that our interests *qua* producers are identical to our interests *qua* citizens. What about interests we might have as consumers? As parents? As religious believers? As members of a particular ethnic or racial group? As residents of a particular locality? As students of world affairs? Citizenship cannot be reduced to an economic category. The young Gramsci's 'producer' democracy was doubtless the perfect embodiment of Marx's assumption that productive labour is the measure of all things; but it also exposed the absurdity of this assumption.

The substitution of communal self-government for worker self-management enables the Marxist to have his cake and eat it—to call for a happy combination of economic regimentation *and* political spontaneity, centralization *and* decentralization. The question must be asked, however: are these compatible goals? The answer is almost certainly no. The problem of combining participatory democracy with national economic planning is diminished but not solved by viewing the local commune as the primary sphere of popular involvement. For if the allocation of resources is to be centrally organized, as it would be in a politically administered economy, then the scope of local democracy will be severely limited. It would not be up to the locality, for example, to determine acceptable levels of pollution from factories in the vicinity, since the production targets of those factories would be authoritatively fixed by the central planning apparatus. Likewise, a standard issue of local democratic debate in market economies—the tax contribution made by local industry to the surrounding community—would have no relevance if the resources of individual productive units were determined by the common plan. Indeed, as all political decisions involve the distribution of material resources, it is difficult to see how any local commune could consistently disregard the dictates of the regional or national or (ultimately) global authority charged with the task of allocating those resources. Given the reality of vertical dependency relations, local autonomy would be a transparent fiction, and Marx's dream of 'self-governing communes'[54] would remain just that—a dream. One can imagine the Marxist rejoinder here: namely, that the plan itself would (or could) accurately reflect the wishes of the people, as expressed through a delegational structure of participatory democracy. Each local council would decide what type of plan it prefers, and the various proposals would be aggregated by the higher elected bodies. At no point would the chain of responsibility and popular control be broken. This picture of the planning process is not entirely fanciful. There is no good reason why the opinions of local communities should be ignored by the higher authorities, as efficient planning requires maximum information about the people's wants and needs. Remember, too, that national policies must be implemented at local level, and unhappy communities are likely to indulge in foot-dragging and other subtle forms of non-co-operation. In areas of special interest, then, local councils might enjoy considerable influence—though not autonomy.

But it is naïve to expect that the central plan can ever be the unadulterated product of some collective will (assuming such a thing exists). Experience tells us that there is an obvious empirical connection between planned economies and overbearing bureaucracies. Is this link necessary or merely contingent? According to Alec Nove, 'given the centralised system, itself the consequence of the elimination of the mar-

---

[54] *The Civil War in France*, 171.

ket, the powerful bureaucracy becomes a functional necessity'.[55] Why? In a market system, decisions about what to
produce are made by consumers themselves, who allocate
their means among the available use-values in the form of
money on the commodities market. Where market regulation
is absent, goods and resources must be allocated according
to objective criteria, enforced by some organ standing above
society. Marx thought that the goals of production could be
established democratically, and that their optimal implementation was merely a technical problem, a matter of efficient administration. In a society of relative scarcity, however,
decisions as to what needs to satisfy, and to what extent,
necessarily depend on technical considerations concerning
their cost. Thus, technical and social decisions cannot be
disentangled, and in practice the means/end distinction
vanishes. Under conditions of total planning, we must conclude, the bureaucratic experts will unavoidably play a major,
maybe even a preponderant role in policy formation, for only
they can conduct the required cost–benefit analysis. At bottom
the power of the bureaucracy would derive from the overwhelming complexity of all-embracing planning. Because of
the vast scale and countless interdependencies of the modern
industrial economy, the task of integration and co-ordination
would be monumentally difficult, the province of skilled spec-
ialists, resistant to anything resembling the detailed democratic control that Marx had in mind. Elected assemblies could,
with the advice of the planners, decide on broad priorities. But
extensive and direct popular participation would find no sustenance in a centralized, vertically structured economy. Ironically, a Marxist could argue otherwise only if he or she
blatantly disregarded the logic of the materialist standpoint.
Selucky is only stating the obvious when he makes the following assertion:

If one accepts Marx's concept of base and superstructure, a centralised
hierarchically organised economic subsystem *cannot* coexist with a
pluralist, horizontally organised self-governed political subsystem. In

---

[55] *The Economics of Feasible Socialism* (London: Allen & Unwin, 1983),
34.

a society with one huge nation-wide factory there is no room either for self-managed economic units or for self-governed communes.[56]

Even in its own terms, Marx's position was fundamentally inconsistent.

Many modern Marxists, curiously undaunted by the difficulties discussed here, remain wedded to a form of radical democracy which 'expresses the right of every individual to participate in making social decisions and to control them directly'.[57] In particular, the idea of worker self-management is favourably contrasted to the (Soviet) model of socialism, where needs are defined from above by central directives, and where the worker is transformed once more into a mere hired hand, no longer of a private employer but of the party/state. The thinkers of the Yugoslav *Praxis* school, for example, believe that the USSR betrayed the essential teachings of Marx. It never seems to occur to these purists that, on the question of democracy, there are intrinsic flaws in Marx's teachings themselves. The Yugoslavs (if the reader will pardon the use of this outmoded but accurate appellation) hold fast to the conviction, inherited from their infallible mentor, that the bureaucratic state was caused by the separation of civil society and the political sphere following the ascent of the bourgeoisie. The alternative (and more obvious) explanation, which pinpoints the irresistible growth and complexity of state functions, is effectively dismissed. Contrary to Weber's thesis, then, bureaucracy is the negation of socialism, not its inevitable expression. The abolition of ' "bossing" by aloof political forces above the working man' is simply a matter of political will.[58]

The posthumous publication of Marx's *Paris Manuscripts* in the 1930s (a body of reflections previously left, as Marx put it, to the 'gnawing criticism of the mice') gave a boost to the exponents of industrial democracy. For these manuscripts con-

[56] R. Selucky, *Marxism, Socialism, Freedom* (London: Macmillan, 1979), 78.
[57] R. Supek, 'The Sociology of Workers' Self-management', in *Self-governing Socialism*, ed. B. Horvat, M. Marković, and R. Supek (White Plains: International Arts and Sciences Press, 1975), 7.
[58] N. Pasić, 'The Idea of Direct Self-managing Democracy and Socialization of Policy-making', in *Self-governing Socialism*, 34–5.

tained Marx's now-famous thoughts on alienation in the work-place. According to this theory (if a few pages of jottings can be so described), the forced expropriation of the product of labour from the producers (i.e. workers), under a system of exploitation, leads to the destruction of their essential crea-tivity. For the worker is estranged not only from his product, but also from the work process, over which he has no control. The capitalist, in order to extract maximum surplus value from his unfortunate hirelings, deploys the latest productive techniques, including an elaborate and spiritually crippling division of labour, marked by repetition and narrow specializa-tion. In the interests of productivity and profit, the worker is treated like a trained gorilla, incapable of initiative or intel-ligent deliberation. Not without justification, the Yugoslavs maintain that if this is Marx's diagnosis, then the remedy must be 'a self-managing productive organization in which the worker directly participates in all essential productive functions'—planning, executing, control, and disposal of the product. Even leaving aside Marx's views on alienation, we can safely assume, say the Yugoslavs, that 'the withering away of the state' meant the replacement of bureaucratic *diktat* by a system of self-managing enterprises. Thus, while acknowledging that Marx was virtually silent about the appro-priate form of industrial democracy, these thinkers insist that workers' self-management is the 'logical consequence' of his critique of bourgeois society.[59] Be that as it may, no one has managed to show how this road to human emancipation could possibly be squared with Marxism's unequivocal rejection of the market mechanism. There is instead a tendency to circum-vent the problem. Marković, to take a notable exemplar of this mode of thought, concedes that a dilemma exists if we focus on man in his present condition, corrupted by 'hunger for consumer goods' and unaware of his 'specific individual powers and potential capacities'. But, through the advent of 'a new socialist culture and a humanist revolution of all educa-tion', there will eventually emerge 'a socialised human being that cares about the needs of other individuals'. At that point,

[59] Supek, 'The Sociology of Workers' Self-management', in *Self-governing Socialism*, 4–5.

planning would in no way conflict with decentralized decision-making, and the 'market economy, with its production for profit,' would be 'replaced by production for genuine human needs'. Society would achieve a dialectical (magical?) synthesis between the universal interests of the general public and the particular interests of different units of production.

All this sounds impeccably democratic until we reflect on the notion of 'genuine human needs'. How are they to be defined? In the short term, at least, it is not a matter of asking people, for

most of what passes under the name of freedom in contemporary society is only illusory freedom: mere opportunity of choice among two or more alternatives. But alternatives are often imposed, choice is arbitrary and even when it has been guided by a consistent criterion of evaluation, this criterion is hardly ever authentic, based on a critical, enlightened examination of one's real needs.

The implication is that democracy must wait (or is at best irrelevant) until the 'humanist revolution of all education' has done its work. We shall wait in vain. It is fatuous to expect some socialist future where everyone's preferences are guided by 'critical, enlightened' analysis, and it is even more fatuous to assume that such analysis would arrive at a single definition of 'real needs'. In an open society, people's values and choices are inevitably influenced by a multiplicity of external forces, and there appears to be no objective method for distinguishing the 'authentic' influences from the 'imposed', 'arbitrary' ones. To dismiss certain needs (or wants) as false is nothing more than an act of stipulation, grounded in a particular conception of 'the good life'. The élitism that Marković has turned away at the front door seems to have sneaked in through the back door. The logical conclusion of his distinction between 'genuine human needs' and 'arbitrary' or false needs is a society where the former are defined from above by benevolent experts, unencumbered by 'hunger for consumer goods'. If Marxist economic planning is a considerable obstacle to participatory democracy, Marxist intellectual élitism is an even bigger one. Marxism was never meant to be a mere theory *of* practice (i.e. the expression in theory of the actual wishes and behaviour of the workers). It is also, and primarily, a theory *for* practice (i.e. objective truth, which the proletariat must adopt as a guide to action). Marxist proponents of participatory democracy oscillate between these two interpretations. Marković is a case in point. In his opinion, 'people themselves must decide about all matters of common interest' but their choices must reflect 'a critical, enlightened examination of one's real needs', which 'practically implies creation of a new socialist culture'.[60] That the people might, after a such an examination, *reject* socialist culture is not, it seems, a possibility that can be contemplated.

This schizophrenic attitude towards the popular will is especially evident in the thought of Rosa Luxemburg, a patron saint of all those Marxists who advocate radically new forms of proletarian democracy. On the one hand, she insisted, against Lenin, that Marxist intellectuals should 'only be the interpreters of the will of the masses'[61]; on the other, she referred to these same intellectuals as 'the most enlightened, most class-conscious *vanguard* of the proletariat'.[62] Such inconsistencies are the legacy of Marx's own ambivalence about the status of his theoretical project. Did Marx see himself as simply a mouthpiece of the working-class struggle? Or did he presume to direct that struggle, in accordance with scientific principles? By way of reply, his texts offer only contradictory pronouncements. Here is a man who, in one and the same paragraph, can assure us that communists 'do not set up any sectarian principles of their own, by which to shape and mold the proletarian movement', but then proceed to laud these very communists as 'the most *advanced* and resolute section of the working class', who have 'the advantage of clearly understanding the line of march, the conditions and the ultimate general results of the proletarian movement'.[63] To describe communists as 'advanced' is of course to hold them up as models for others to emulate. Yet Marx also

[60] M. Marković, 'Self-management and Efficiency', in *The Contemporary Marx: Essays on Humanist Communism* (Nottingham: Spokesman Books, 1974), 211–12.

[61] *The Mass Strike, the Political Party and the Trade Unions*, first pub. 1906 (London: Merlin Press, n. d.), 85.

[62] Ibid. 64, my emphasis.

[63] *Manifesto of the Communist Party*, in *Marx & Engels: Basic Writings*, 20, my emphasis.

gainsaid any desire to 'shape' the movement to suit his own principles. One can forgive the confusion of those who tried to follow in his footsteps. In common with all great reformers, he vacillated between admitting rationality as a general attribute of human beings and ascribing a privileged role to radical intellectuals and experts.

Marx's more orthodox disciples implicitly conceded the existence of a dilemma: they by and large recognized that direct or participatory forms of democracy (whatever their inherent value) cut against the grain of Marxism's rationalizing and centralizing mission. In the absence of viable alternatives some, like Kautsky, discovered hidden virtues in the very parliamentary system that Marx so despised. When purged of its bourgeois content, this model could, they believed, express 'the self-determination of the people'.

III   The Parliamentary Model

Prior to becoming an outspoken critic of Bolshevism in 1918, Kautsky was held in great esteem as an authoritative interpreter of Marx's thought. Even those who disagreed with his suspiciously tame political conclusions had to admit that his philosophical and economic premises were the epitome of orthodoxy. However, his understanding of Marxism as a form of materialist evolutionism owed more to Engels than to Marx himself, who maintained a baffling silence on how the historical dialectic relates to the material world. A number of commentators have pointed out that Marx's own writings are not concerned with metaphysical questions about the primal substance, and that he never explicitly endorsed a 'substantialist' belief in matter as the substratum of all that can meaningfully be said to exist.[64] Indeed, these commentators are fond of quoting certain passages (from his early works)

---

[64] See, for example, L. Kolakowski, *Main Currents of Marxism*, vol. i, *The Founders* (Oxford: Oxford University Press, 1981), ch. 16; G. Lichtheim, *Marxism* (London: Routledge and Kegan Paul, 1961), Pt. 5, ch. 4; and Avineri, *The Social and Political Thought of Karl Marx*, ch. 3. This interpretation traces its ancestry back to Georgy Lukács. See, in particular, his essay 'What is Orthodox Marxism?', in *History and Class Consciousness* (Cambridge, Mass.: MIT Press, 1971).

where his assignment of a constitutive role to conscious human activity would seem to contradict the reduction of all reality to material objects and processes. Marx, on this view, actually *opposed* the materialist metaphysics of Engels. Whether the evidence is sufficient to prove such a claim is doubtful.[65] All we can say for certain is that it was Engels, not Marx, who developed the 'dialectic of nature'. While the details of this exegetical controversy need not detain us, I do wish to argue that the success of Engels (and Kautsky) in aligning Marxism with naturalistic materialism may help to account for the willingness of some Marxists to embrace the basic postulates of liberal democratic theory and practice.

No one can deny that, with the publication of his *Anti-Dühring* in 1877, Engels made a profound contribution to Marxist philosophy. Although he never pretended to be more than a faithful interpreter of his friend's teachings, Engels was undoubtedly responsible for transforming Marxism into a coherent cosmic synthesis that presumed to explain everything, from the most elementary biological level right up to the level of human history. His dialectic was formulated in the intellectual atmosphere of Darwinism, and he attempted, with or without Marx's blessing, to incorporate Darwin's theory into the Marxist framework. Starting from the assumption that man is an object in nature, whose thought processes are nothing but chemical secretions within the brain, Engels concluded that human history was simply an extension of natural history, and therefore subject to the same laws. The development of mankind was seen as a causally determined process analogous to the Darwinian scheme of evolution. This 'interpretation' of Marxian doctrine might more accurately be described as a subtle revision. For Marx, in his own fashion, had borrowed from Hegel the idea of history culminating in a unique breakthrough: the identification of man's existence with his species essence. Even in Marx's later writings, we find the substance, if not the language, of Hegelian teleology. But this revolutionary eschatology appears to be ruled out if, following Engels, we construe history as an evolutionary pat-

---

[65] For a detailed and scholarly denial of the alleged division between Marx and Engels, see J. Hoffman, *Marxism and the Theory of Praxis* (London: Lawrence and Wishart, 1975), 47–56.

tern obeying the laws of material necessity. For nature can never reach a 'climax' and thus cannot yield up any definite meaning. In the words of George Lichtheim:

Nature is immortal almost by definition, and its study—as Engels never tires of stressing—discloses no finality, but at best an endless approximation to a constantly receding limit. To assimilate the historical process to that of nature consequently means doing away with the idea of a decisive historical act that reveals the *meaning* of history.[66]

The logic of Engels's model dictates that history, like nature, is a succession of law-governed physical events, with no immanent essence. But if this is so, if there is no final state, no inherent purpose, just infinite progression, with (as in external nature) one form developing organically out of another, then it is not at all clear why anyone should posit a sharp division, a complete break, between the present order and that which is to come. To be sure, once Marxism came to be identified with materialist cosmology, the messianic promise of an ideal era of human perfection began to fade into the background. Karl Korsch, one of the original Marxist 'humanists', was an acute observer and critic of this trend. With Kautsky in his sights, he rightly argued that the 'pseudo-Darwinian metaphysics of evolution' assumed the 'complete determination' of higher stages by lower ones. Communism thus becomes 'a further developed form of bourgeois society' rather than 'a new type which is no longer to be basically explained by any of the bourgeois categories'.[67] What Korsch considered a weakness, however, might more plausibly be deemed a strength; for Engels's (and Kautsky's) naturalistic interpretation of the human condition completed the Marxian project of bringing philosophy down to earth—something Marx himself never quite achieved. His vestigial Utopianism, which mocked his pretensions to scientific rigour, was logically incompatible with the evolutionary materialism of his successors. Their mental universe could not, strictly speaking, accommodate preconceived schemes for an ideal society, counterposed to reality and valid from here to eternity. Flights

---

[66] *Marxism*, 250–1.
[67] *Three Essays on Marxism* (London: Pluto Press, 1971), 34–6. The essays were first published (in German) in the 1930s.

of democratic fancy, splendid visions of ubiquitous citizen—legislators—administrators—these residues of 'Utopian socialism' had no discernible basis in the empirical world. Quite the reverse. Nor could a consistent materialist grant them any special metaphysical status.

Kautsky, to his credit, was prepared to admit as much. Deeply pessimistic about the self-administrative powers of the working class, he rejected the Leninist contrast between a proletarian democracy founded on soviets, and a bourgeois democracy founded on parliamentarism. He did not believe that the liberal state had to be 'smashed', as Marx and Lenin demanded, or that the parliamentary system had to be replaced by a fusion of legislative and executive powers, or that bureaucracy had to be dismantled as a professionally organized institution. Such demands were, to his mind, totally unrealistic. It was a lesson of historical experience, he maintained, that direct democracy, as well as the anti-centralism associated with it, were firmly rooted in the past. Both were doomed to extinction in a society dominated by large-scale industry, by productive methods whose perpetuation required not only central planning and co-ordination but also a professionally selected technical apparatus.[68] Participatory democracy, whether in its communal or industrial form, clashed with the modern need for expertise. '[P]ublic affairs', Kautsky wrote in the 1890s, 'are today too complicated, too manifold, and too wide-ranging to be dealt with by amateurs working in their spare time.' We must therefore rely upon 'expert and trained people, paid functionaries who dedicate themselves to such tasks completely'. The idea of a 'government of the people and by the people in the sense that public affairs should be administered not by functionaries but by the popular masses', working without pay on a part-time basis, is 'a utopia, even a reactionary and anti-democratic utopia, no matter how many democrats and revolutionaries may champion it'.[69] People like Pannekoek,

---

[68] K. Kautsky, *The Class Struggle*, trans. W. E. Bohn (New York: W. W. Norton, 1971), 100–1. This book was written in 1892 as a general statement of the articles of belief of the German Social Democratic Party (SPD), then the largest and most influential Marxist party in Europe.

[69] K. Kautsky, *La questione agraria* (Milan: Feltrinelli, 1959), 473. This work was originally published in German; there is no English edition.

we are told, seem to forget that the purpose of socialism is to *extend* the public sector—indeed, 'the enormous task of regulating the gigantic mechanism of production of our era will ... devolve upon the state'. And the 'more extensive and complex the state apparatus becomes, the more do those responsible for managing it and putting it to use have need of special knowledge'.[70] We cannot dispense with bureaucrats and professional politicians, those with a 'special vocation' to discharge the nation's business. With reluctance, Kautsky accepts that, as public affairs become more technical, the citizen's sphere of competence shrinks. The chief protagonist of industrial society (particularly in its socialist form) is the expert; the chief protagonist of democratic society is the ordinary man-in-the-street. It follows that the very notion of industrial democracy is problematic. Notwithstanding the hopes and dreams of radical Marxists, there is bound to be a conflict between participation and efficiency. To accede to the demands of Pannekoek and his supporters is to ignore the objective conditions of modern life. Economic ruin would be the inexorable consequence.

But, in Kautsky's opinion, council communism was not only deficient in a technical sense; it was also politically deficient. A council system, especially if based in the workplace, would exalt particularistic tendencies, creating and consolidating divisively local interests and loyalties. The self-administered society would be inherently fissiparous. In parliamentary elections, on the other hand, diverse social interests are aggregated and homogenized by political parties, whose national structure enables them to develop an overview of public needs and capacities. Council communism would impede national, not to mention rational, co-ordination of policy.[71] Furthermore, if this new system involved the unity of legislative and executive powers, despotic temptations would be hard to resist. A division of powers is intrinsically safer, for 'history shows us that an assembly that commands both the executive and legislative power does not

---

[70] K. Kautsky, *The Materialist Conception of History*, trans. R. Meyer and J. H. Kautsky (New Haven, Conn.: Yale University Press, 1988), 387, 448. Originally published in 1927.

[71] M. Salvadori, *Karl Kautsky and the Socialist Revolution: 1880–1938*, trans. J. Rothschild (London: New Left Books, 1979), 226–45.

brook the slightest opposition'.[72] Bear in mind, says Kautsky, that executive tasks require action, whose condition is maximum unity, which active opposition would tend to destroy. By contrast, the legislative function works best if every law emerges from a confrontation of conflicting opinions. To unify these two powers is to combine (or attempt to combine) two mutually exclusive principles. In practice one or the other would have to give way. And experience tells us that the principle of cohesion would triumph at the expense of unfettered debate, because the opposite solution would bring administrative chaos.[73]

By no means was Kautsky arguing that parliamentary government *as then practised* represented the summit of man's political aspiration. Centralization, he believed, should be tempered with controls exercised by powerful local bodies, including consumer associations (to counteract socialism's inherent bias towards producers) and elected assemblies at regional, district, and municipal levels. Even factory councils would have a role to play, though they could not become organs of state power or presume to overrule central economic decisions.[74] Kautsky's thoughts on the devolution of power remained ill-defined. Like all Marxists, he was more concerned with the defects of capitalism than with the details of the future society. Still, on the main issue he was always crystal clear: parliamentary democracy 'constitutes the indispensable political foundation of the new collective order', and those who say otherwise inhabit that domain where the wish is father to the thought.[75] Their conception of communism, innocent of economic and politicial realities, was destined to remain a 'mere idealized abstraction'.[76]

It would seem, then, that Kautsky abandoned all hope of the state withering away or of popular self-organization (however conceived) taking its place. Appearances can be deceptive, however. For he never denied that the *coercive apparatus* of

---

[72] Ibid. 276 (quotation taken from a pamphlet entitled *Die proletarische revolution und ihr programm*, which was a commentary on the SPD programme adopted at its Congress in 1921).

[73] Ibid.

[74] Ibid. 231–3.

[75] Quoted ibid. 232.

[76] Quoted ibid. 159.

the state would eventually disappear. But he did insist that Engels was wrong to describe communism as some kind of spontaneous order where 'the government of persons is replaced by the administration of things'. This formula, Kautsky observes, presents a false dichotomy, since administering things invariably requires the direction of people. The real contrast is between domination and persuasion, coercion and consent. Perhaps, he concludes, one should speak not of 'the withering away of the state' but of its 'change of function'.[77]

According to Kautsky, too many Marxists were led astray by a misguided, almost mystical belief in some distinctively 'proletarian' mode of democracy. In his view, democracy did not come with class labels; it simply referred to a set of principles and procedures—constitutionalism, universal suffrage, civil rights, representation, division of powers—whose primary purpose was to guarantee majority rule. Although he readily agreed that the existing regime was 'a power apparatus in the service of the ruling and exploiting classes for the repression of the ruled and exploited', he emphatically denied that this function was derived from the 'idea' of the liberal state.[78] Whether or not parliamentary democracy served the interests of this or that class should be determined by empirical investigation, not by appeals to some abstract essence. Where the liberal state becomes an instrument of an exploitative minority, this is due 'not to the nature of the state but to the nature of the working classes, to their lack of unity, their ignorance, dependency, or inability to fight'.[79] Through the experience of economic and political struggle, however, the proletariat can (and will) 'turn the apparatus of domination into an apparatus of emancipation'.[80] The seizure of power means nothing other than winning a majority within parliament, and this triumph is assured by the internal contradictions of capitalism, a system whose bankruptcy leaves socialism as the only realistic alternative. Neither bullets nor bayonets can stop what is inherent in 'the logic of things': 'The time and manner of its accomplishment may vary in

---

[77] *The Materialist Conception of History*, 448–9.
[78] Ibid. 266–7.
[79] Ibid. 444.
[80] Ibid. 387. See also *The Class Struggle*, 188.

different lands, but there can be no doubt as to the final victory of the proletariat.'[81] Kautsky's boundless faith in the historical dialectic doubtless encouraged his optimism about a peaceful transition via the ballot box. But the key factor in his espousal of the 'parliamentary road' was his faith in the essential classlessness of democratic institutions.

Kautsky was an unusual Marxist in as much as his basic instincts were liberal. He also had a keen eye for faulty logic and doctrinal cant, which made him suspicious of all those who treated Marx's works as Holy Writ. As we saw earlier, he refused to dismiss civil rights as 'formal' or 'bourgeois'. If people actually do vote and express themselves freely through press and parliament, how, he asks, can these rights be deemed 'formal'? And if a socialist uses his freedom to make a speech attacking bourgeois society, in what sense is he exercising a 'bourgeois' right? Kautsky accused his Marxist opponents of making a fundamental logical error: that because parliamentary democratic practices do not lead to the *immediate* abolition of all exploitation, they must be part and parcel of the repressive capitalist system. This, for him, was an obvious *non sequitur*.[82]

For the most part, Kautsky passed in silence over the apparent differences between his own ideas and those of Marx. In the face of Bolshevik dictatorship, however, he felt obliged to defend the orthodoxy of his liberal predilections. Events in Russia confirmed what he had always suspected: that all the lofty rhetoric about councils and new forms of democracy masked the intention to set up a minority despotism. In *The Dictatorship of the Proletariat*, a pamphlet published in 1918, he mounted a devastating attack on the emergent 'soviet' regime. To begin with, he pointed to the absurdity of pretending that the working class now governed Russia, 'for a class is a shapeless mass and only an organisation can govern'. In fact, the Bolshevik Party governed Russia. No party, moreover, could claim to speak for a whole class, since 'the same class interest may be represented in very diverse ways by means of different tactical procedures, and on the basis of such different

---

[81] *The Class Struggle*, 189.
[82] *The Materialist Conception of History*, 374–5.

tactics the representatives of identical class interests split up
into different parties'. Thus, 'party and class do not necessarily
coincide'. What Bolshevism amounted to was dictatorship by
a party masquerading as dictatorship by a class. If Lenin were
serious about proletarian rule, he would encourage a multi-
party system, in which different parties purporting to represent
the majority interest would have their claims tested in free
electoral competition. But once we acknowledge the need for
competitive democratic politics, we must also accept the standard liberal guarantees—in particular, the protection of minorities, of their freedom to organize and oppose.[83] Kautsky was
alarmed by the Bolsheviks' brutal treatment of their opponents, as evidenced by the dissolution of the Constituent
Assembly in January of 1918 and the subsequent restriction of
representation in the soviets according to class criteria. It was
dishonest of Lenin and his colleagues, Kautsky alleged, to
hide behind those passages where Marx justified a transitional
'dictatorship' before the advent of 'stateless' communism.[84]
For he did not intend 'dictatorship in the literal sense', a
repressive *'form of government'*, but rather '*a state of affairs*
which must necessarily arise wherever the proletariat achieves
political power' through its overwhelming numerical strength.
Dictatorship, so construed, in no way entails suppression of
opposition, suspension of freedom of the press and association,
or the denial of the franchise to opponents. Did Marx not
praise the Paris Commune, which was based on universal
suffrage and free elections? Had not Engels expressly held up
the Commune as the first example of 'the dictatorship of the
proletariat'? In any case, Marx could hardly have had a 'form
of government' in mind, as dictatorship in this sense would
have to be of a party or perhaps a small group, whereas he of
course referred to the dictatorship of the proletariat.[85]

While Marx was vague about the details of the dictatorship,
most commentators agree that he had no intention of justify-
ing *minority* rule. But it is equally true that neither he nor

---

[83] *Karl Kautsky: Selected Political Writings*, ed. and trans. P. Goode
(London: Macmillan, 1983), 110–11.

[84] See, e.g., 'Critique of the Gotha Program', in *Marx & Engels: Basic
Writings* , 127.

[85] *Karl Kautsky: Selected Political Writings*, 114–16.

Engels showed much respect for liberal constitutional safe-guards. Writing in 1875, for example, the latter declared that the purpose of *any* state is 'to hold down one's adversaries by force'.[86] In his influential essay 'On Authority', he portrayed revolution as

certainly the most authoritarian thing there is; it is the act whereby one part of the population imposes its will upon the other part by means of rifles, bayonets and cannon—authoritarian means if such there be at all; and if the victorious party does not want to have fought in vain, it must maintain this rule by means of the terror which its arms inspire in the reactionaries.[87]

Likewise Marx, in a letter of 1881, stated that 'the first *desideratum*' of a socialist government is to 'take the necessary measures for intimidating the mass of the bourgeoisie'.[88] Protection of minority rights formed no part of the Marx–Engels world-view, their attachment to participatory democracy notwithstanding.

Lenin hammered home this very point in his venomous rejoinder to Kautsky, where he accused his former idol of becoming a 'sentimental simpleton', 'belly-crawling and boot-licking before the bourgeoisie'.[89] The Russian leader made plain his contempt for liberal pieties. From the proletarian standpoint, parliament was an 'alien' institution and soviet government was 'a million times more democratic than the most democratic bourgeois republic'. Kautsky, in defending parliamentarism, in attempting to revive a 'stinking corpse', was depriving Marxism 'of its revolutionary living soul'. To define democracy from 'the formal legal point of view', while 'ignoring the class struggle', amounted to 'the adoption of the bourgeois point of view'.[90] Though one would never know it from reading this diatribe against the 'renegade' Kautsky, the political significance of money and property, along with the political partiality of state action, were not in dispute between

[86] K. Marx and F. Engels, *Selected Correspondence: 1846–1895* (New York: International Publishers, 1942), 337.

[87] *Marx & Engels: Basic Writings*, 485.

[88] *Selected Correspondence*, 386.

[89] V. I. Lenin, *The Proletarian Revolution and the Renegade Kautsky* (London: Martin Lawrence, 1935), 28, 35.

[90] Ibid. 11, 30, 59, 100.

him and Lenin. What was at issue was the emancipatory potential of parliamentary democracy. Thus were the battle lines drawn in the struggle for Marxism's 'living soul'.

The Russian revolution gave the Bolsheviks the power and prestige to dominate world Marxism, and by the 1920s friend and foe alike had come to assume that Marxist 'democracy' was precisely what Lenin, and later Stalin, said it was. Kautsky was branded a traitor, a purveyor of revisionist claptrap, unfit for Marxist consumption. As we have already seen, however, his benign attitude towards parliamentary principles and institutions was resurrected in the 1970s by a new breed of 'Marxists': the so-called Eurocommunists, whose ideas merit some discussion here. But in order to understand the phenomenon or Eurocommunism, we must first uncover its historical origins in post-fascist Italy, the country that spawned the largest of all Western communist parties.

As the Second World War drew to a close, the Italian Communist Party (PCI) began to define and pursue a *'terza via al socialismo'*, a third road to socialism, attuned to post-war conditions and supposedly distinct from the practices of either orthodox Leninism or conventional social democracy. As was the case in other parts of Europe, notably France, the admirable record of communists within the Resistance movement had earned the PCI a great deal of popular support; and even before the victory over fascism was complete, the Party sought, under the leadership of Palmiro Togliatti, to consolidate its gains by presenting itself as a patriotic mass organization, committed to electoral politics. Initially, this unthreatening posture had Stalin's approval, for it reflected his wish to mollify the Allies and win acceptance for his virtual annexation of Eastern Europe. In any event, the United States was not about to tolerate a communist revolution in a country it had just liberated from Nazi occupation. In the political deliberations of the PCI, necessity was very much the mother of invention.

In a celebrated speech to the newly liberated people of Naples in April 1944, Togliatti offered the first statement of the *terza via*. He made it clear that the immediate objective of his party was not socialism but 'a democratic and progressive regime', which would carry out the 'great national function of recovery, reconciliation and renewal of the whole of Italian life'.[91] The hallmark of the new strategy was national unity: collaboration with other political parties and social classes to achieve economic reconstruction and create a democratic political order that would facilitate a gradual transition to socialism. Acutely aware of the PCI's minority status in a Catholic, largely agrarian country, Togliatti warned against the dangers of isolation: 'We can no longer be a small, tightly knit association of propagandists. . . . We have to be a big party, a mass party', reaching out beyond its traditional constituency to embrace a wide variety of anti-fascist forces, from peasants and intellectuals to the 'productive bourgeoisie' —artisans, clerical and professional workers, even small industrialists. This would be a 'party of unity', with no room for 'exclusivist and sectarian narrowmindedness'.[92] Even so, the new regime could not be 'based on the existence or the domination of one sole party'. Communism was not the only legitimate political movement. It was therefore desirable to form alliances with progressive Catholics and liberals who, like the PCI, opposed 'big monoply capitalism' and wished to build a 'new Italy'.[93] Since the dominant motif was collaboration, Togliatti's strategy required proletarian 'responsibility' and a moderation of economic demands. For the time being, the Party would press for nothing more radical than nationalization of the 'commanding heights' of the economy, together with strategic planning and agrarian reform.

The *terza via*, in its embryonic phase, was evocative of the 'Popular Front' strategy of the 1930s, whose purpose was to mobilize a broad alliance of anti-fascist forces around the intermediate goal of restoring bourgeois democracy. In those dark days, Marxist militancy was temporarily suspended, as the hand of friendship (or at least co-operation) was extended to all social groups, save for the representatives of finance and monopoly capital, who were considered the bedrock of fascism. There was, however, a subtle difference between the Popular Front approach and Togliatti's proposals, for the 'pro-

---

[91] *On Gramsci and Other Writings*, ed. and trans. D. Sassoon (London: Lawrence and Wishart, 1979), 39, 58.
[92] Ibid. 42, 61–2.
[93] Ibid. 40, 58.

gressive' democracy envisaged by the latter would not be bourgeois in the customary sense of the term. On the contrary, it would incorporate certain elements of socialism. Yet, in his speeches of 1944 and 1945, Togliatti conveyed the impression that 'the reconstruction and rebirth of Italy'[94] could be achieved in the absence of anything resembling a revolutionary break. Combining stealth and imagination in equal measure, he set off on a new path to socialism. And what started out as a small, uncharted detour eventually became the grand *via Italiana*, proudly reflecting national qualities and traditions rather than the whims of Moscow. But for many years, the 'third road' was strewn with pitfalls, and its negotiation required some fancy footwork on the part of Togliatti.

Like so many of his fellow southern Italians, the PCI leader was a verbal gymnast of the highest order, somehow managing to define his heterodox strategy without alienating either his Russian backers or the more neanderthal members of his own rank-and-file. In order to reassure the Leninists at home and abroad, he undertook to invest the new Party image with Gramscian paternity. Gramsci, an illustrious figure in the communist pantheon, who died during his incarceration by Mussolini's regime, had acquired special heroic status, especially in Italy, because of his martyrdom in the struggle against fascism. From his *Prison Notebooks*, Togliatti claimed to derive both inspiration and practical instruction. The present writer has already examined this claim in considerable detail, and there is no need to rehearse my arguments here.[95] Suffice it to point out that Gramsci's scattered remarks about a fresh approach to revolution in advanced capitalist societies provided a plausible basis for Togliatti's policy. As a consistent adversary of dogmatic internationalism and tactical inflexibility, Gramsci did indeed urge communist parties to adapt to peculiar national conditions and circumstances. Moreover, it was central to his analysis that revolution in the West could never be successful unless preceded by a protracted 'war of position', a battle to win the 'hearts and minds' of the vast

---

[94] Speech delivered at Florence in Oct. 1944, ibid. 75.
[95] Femia, *Gramsci's Political Thought*, ch. 6.

majority. The immediate goal, as depicted in the *Notebooks*, was to establish a Marxist 'presence' in all the institutions of 'civil society': schools, mass media, trade unions, universities, publishing houses, even churches. The experience of fascism, combined with the international proletariat's passive response to the Great Depression, had convinced Gramsci that the revolutionary process in the West would be a long march, requiring intermediate aims and strategies. He was alive to the need for class alliances, for caution and short-term compromises, for the construction of a national consensus around socialist values and principles. On the other hand, he felt sure that the 'war of position' would have to be complemented by a 'war of manœuvre'—i.e. revolutionary militancy and eventual insurrection; and he never indicated the slightest sympathy for Kautsky's view that parliamentary democracy would (and should) outlive the capitalist mode of production. Togliatti, in the immediate aftermath of Italy's liberation, wisely chose to disregard the strictly Leninist side of his late colleague's thought. His Gramsci was a prophet of national unity in the task of anti-fascist resistance and democratic renewal:

The central idea of Gramsci's political activity was unity: unity of the working-class parties in the struggle to defend democratic institutions ... unity of the working-class parties with the democratic forces which were beginning to organize ... unity of the socialist working masses with the Catholic working masses ... unity of workers and peasants; unity of workers of the arm with those of the mind, for the creation of a great bloc of national forces.[96]

These words were part of a speech delivered in 1945 to the comrades of Naples. But the start of the Cold War in 1947 demanded an abrupt change of rhetoric, if not policy, and PCI language reverted to classical themes of class conflict as well as confrontation with the Catholic Church. Gramsci was now presented as a Leninist—a 'creative' one, certainly, but a Leninist none the less. Stalin was no longer in a mood to countenance talk of broad alliances or 'progressive democracy'. In the bleak atmosphere of East–West conflict and anti-

---

[96] Speech delivered at Naples in Apr. 1945. Reprinted in *Rinascita*, 29 Aug. 1964, pp. 15–17.

communist hysteria, Togliatti was forced to walk a tightrope, balancing the dictates of Moscow with the need to establish the PCI as a *partito di governo*, as a legitimate actor within the Italian political system. Deviations from orthodoxy were usually cloaked in the familiar Leninist idiom and counterpoised by fulsome pledges of allegiance to the USSR, which he described in 1956 as 'superior in quality to present-day capitalist states'.[97] For the most part, however, the actual practice of the Party did not change, and it never used its parliamentary presence or grass-roots power to make the country ungovernable. Continued adherence to Leninism and the Soviet mystique served, as one commentator observes, 'more as a fiction to reinforce party identity than as a strategic guide to action'.[98]

By 1956 the Soviets were themselves reassessing Stalin's legacy. In an earthquaking speech, delivered in February of that year to the Twentieth Congress of the CPSU, Khrushchev, the Party Chairman, gave a detailed account of Stalin's horrendous crimes and paranoid delusions. Togliatti, emboldened by the resulting climate of doubt and criticism, was now prepared to make explicit what had already been implicit in the PCI's *modus operandi*. His views were famously expressed in a lengthy interview given to the journal *Nuovi Argomenti*. The pursuit of world socialism, he declared, was 'becoming polycentric' and further progress meant 'following roads which are often different'. Each communist party should respond to its own country's unique configuration of values, conventions, and social forces. There was no universal formula for realizing the good society. Attempts to impose socialism through a set of ready-made prescriptions would lead to 'bureaucratic degeneration, ... the suffocation of democratic life, ... and the destruction of revolutionary legality'. These remarks, though hedged about with tributes to the heroic and world-historic achievements of the USSR, betrayed profound misgivings about Soviet 'democracy', which, the PCI boss implied, had become detached from 'the creative activity of the masses'.[99]

---

[97] *On Gramsci and Other Writings*, 118.

[98] C. Boggs, 'The Democratic Road: New Departures and Old Problems', in *The Politics of Eurocommunism*, ed. C. Boggs and D. Plotke (London: Macmillan, 1980), 433.

[99] *On Gramsci and Other Writings*, 141–2.

Significantly, however, he denied that the one-party state was inherently undemocratic, since 'the dialectic of contradiction' could express itself 'right inside the single system'.[100]

In his final text, known as the 'Yalta Memorandum' (published just before his death in 1964), Togliatti edged further away from orthodoxy by effectively endorsing Kautsky's defence of parliaments and civil liberties. It might be possible, he conceded, 'for the working classes to win positions of power within the limits of a state that has not changed its bourgeois nature' and therefore 'to struggle for the progressive transformation of its nature from the inside'. Parliament, it seemed, could have a greater or lesser degree of democratic representativeness and legitimacy. He also expressed his disapproval of the dogmatism and repression that had marred the Soviet experiment. Communists 'must become the champions of the freedom of intellectual life, of free artistic creation, and of scientific progress'. Rather than 'abstractly counterpose our conception to different tendencies and currents', the intelligent Marxist should aim for 'reciprocal understanding, won through a continuous debate'.[101] In this, his political last will and testament, Togliatti was simply pursuing the implications of his 'polycentrism'.

The Yalta Memorandum became a major point of reference in the subsequent development of the *via Italiana*. Togliatti himself, possibly out of loyalty and sentiment, always paid ritual obeisance to the idea of a world communist movement (albeit diversified) with Moscow as its heart and soul. His successors, by comparison, saw no need to apply eulogistic epithets to the USSR. To their minds, *world* communism was a dead letter and there was little point in pretending otherwise. Leninist rhetoric became conspicuous by its absence, as polycentrism was taken to its logical conclusion: open criticism of Soviet monism together with a forthright attachment to Western pluralism. The 'Italian road' furnished the model for what came to be known as Eurocommunism, itself merely a codification of established ideas and practices. Apart from the PCI, there were two other significant communist parties in the West, those of Spain (PCE) and France (PCF), both of

---

[100] Ibid. 122.
[101] Ibid. 292–3.

which had already changed their Stalinist ways by the early 1970s. After a meeting held in Madrid in March 1977, the three General Secretaries (Enrico Berlinguer of the PCI, Georges Marchais of the PCF, and Santiago Carrillo of the PCE) issued a joint statement declaring their respect for 'the pluralism of political and social forces' and guaranteeing the protection 'of all individual and collective freedoms', including 'the inviolability of private life'.[102] Thus was Eurocommunism born. Such liberal sentiments, so loudly proclaimed, were certain to disturb Lenin's eternal sleep. But, as Carrillo said in his lengthy defence of the democratic path, Bolshevik methods 'are not applicable today because they have been overtaken in the circumstances of the developed capitalist countries'.[103]

For purposes of analysis, Eurocommunism can be divided into five basic principles or theses:

(i) Use of the forms and practices of 'bourgeois' democracy as the fundamental means of achieving power and building socialism. Violence and insurrectionary upheaval are dismissed as inappropriate in Western Europe, where 'bourgeois democracy was born, where representative institutions have a more or less strong tradition'.[104] The Eurocommunists, echoing Togliatti's doctrine of polycentrism, insist that roads to socialism must correspond to the conditions and circumstances specific to each country. Strategies that might succeed in backward or despotic lands have no validity in advanced countries where liberalism and capitalism enjoy the active consent of the majority. It is necessary, as Gramsci argued, to subvert this consensus through ideological combat. If this struggle is successful, say the Eurocommunists, Marxists will be able to use their parliamentary majority to transform society through peaceful and constitutional methods. Change would be evolutionary, not revolutionary. And since bourgeois power structures can be dismantled through existing state institutions

[102] *L'Unità*, 4 March 1977.
[103] S. Carrillo, *Eurocommunism and the State* (Westport, Conn.: Lawrence Hill, 1978), 10.
[104] *The Italian Road to Socialism*, an interview by E. Hobsbawm with G. Napolitano, chief economic spokesman of the Italian Communist Party (Westport: Lawrence Hill, 1977), 78.

(parliament, the bureaucratic apparatus, the judiciary), there is no need to destroy these institutions. Suitably reformed, they can remain as integral components of the socialist future. The Eurocommunists are at one with Kautsky in seeing the liberal state as an adaptable instrument, capable of being used by the leftist opposition as well as by the ruling class.

(ii) The transformation of society proceeds through a series of 'profound structural transformations', designed to increase popular control of economic and political life.[105] The eventual aim is to socialize 'the decisive levers of the economy' and to institute 'democratic planning, on a national scale'.[106] This 'democratic planning' would involve 'the participation of the working class, occupying a determining position, in planning decisions at all levels from below and from above'.[107] By no means should planning be seen 'as something bureaucratically imposed'.[108] As with Kautsky, there would be a role for workers' councils, though not at the expense of economic or political rationality. Where Eurocommunists differ from Kautsky is in their acceptance of a permanent (if restricted) place for both market regulation (to complement planning) and private enterprise (especially small, family-based industries).[109] Still, it is repeatedly stressed that 'the collective interest must prevail in the determination of the direction of the country's economic and social development'.[110] Unlike conventional social democrats, the Eurocommunists by and large accept the orthodox Marxist view that the 'anarchic' nature of capitalism, caused by untamed market forces, prevents the fullest utilization of productive capabilities.[111] The 'objective contradictions inherent in the mode of capitalist production' are, we learn, crying out for a socialist solution. On the political level, there would have to be 'a whole series of modifications' in the 'structure and functioning of the state machinery, aiming fundamentally at decentralization,

---

[105] Ibid. 77.
[106] Carrillo, *Eurocommunism and the State*, 77–8.
[107] *The Italian Road to Socialism*, 52.
[108] Carrillo, *Eurocommunism and the State*, 78.
[109] Ibid. 80; *The Italian Road to Socialism*, 52.
[110] *The Italian Road to Socialism*, 52.
[111] Ibid. 92; Carrillo, *Eurocommunism and the State*, 46; and E. Berlinguer, *La proposta comunista* (Turin: Einaudi, 1975), 7, 145.

developing regional and local autonomy, popular participation and control'.[112] In agreement with Kautsky, Eurocommunists believe in a balance between centralization and decentralization, and see no necessary incompatibility between national economic planning and greater citizen involvement in the decision-making process.[113] But, also like Kautsky, they are less than specific about the precise institutional forms of this 'direct participation'.[114]

(iii) The pursuit of structural reforms necessitates an imaginative search for alliances with any or all social and political forces that are (potentially) opposed to the big monopolies and the multinational corporations. Coalitions with non-socialist parties should not be shunned, and special attention should be devoted to the expanding middle strata (civil servants, professionals, technicians, small businessmen) as possible recruits to a reformed communism. Bowing to the exigencies of modern technological society, with its blurred class structure and increasing reliance on mental labour, the Eurocommunists acknowledge that progressive political change cannot be brought about by an exclusively working-class party acting on its own. The old Marxist politics of confrontation, ridiculed as a relic from a bygone era, yields pride of place to the 'politics of unity'.[115]

(iv) A corollary of the quest for consensus is the recognition of ideological and cultural diversity as a legitimate and valuable aspect of the future order. Otherwise stated, Eurocommunism is committed to pluralism at all levels of social life. This entails abandonment of the vanguard theory of the party (though the PCF has been less forthright than the other parties in dropping the Leninist inheritance). In the opinion of a PCI spokesman, 'ideas which assign to the Communist Party an exclusive leadership role in the process of transforming the society in a socialist direction must be completely and definitively overcome'.[116] It is essential to avoid a situation where, in the words of Jean Elleinstein, an influential French com-

---

[112] *The Italian Road to Socialism*, 50.
[113] Carrillo, *Eurocommunism and the State*, 75–6.
[114] *The Italian Road to Socialism*, 84.
[115] Berlinguer, *La proposta comunista*, 101, 138–9.
[116] *The Italian Road to Socialism*, 78.

munist intellectual, 'State and Party coincide'.[117] Similarly, Carrillo admits that the Communist Party has no 'providential mission ... entrusted by the grace of our teachers or through some authorisation from on high'. Thus communists should not seek to impose their ideology or establish it as an official creed. Indeed, the party must jettison its 'scientific' claim to be the sole bearer of *working class* interests, let alone those of society as a whole.[118]

(v) The acceptance of pluralism and the apparatus of the liberal state makes little sense unless accompanied by a commitment to preserve constitutional rights and liberties, including those of political opposition. The position here is not distant from that of Kautsky: such rights and liberties, though limited in effectiveness by their bourgeois context, provide oxygen for the anti-monopoly forces and merit a permanent place in the future order. Carrillo, for example, calls for 'a socialism which would maintain and enrich the democratic political liberties and human rights which are historic achievements of human progress'; while Napolitano promises 'respect for the rights of the opposition and the alternation of majority and minority in a parliamentary dialectic'.[119] Eurocommunists are therefore prepared, as Elleinstein puts it, 'to abide by the rules of parliamentary democracy and relinquish the levers of power if they lose the confidence of the public'.[120] Whereas Togliatti seemed to look upon the multi-party system as a necessary evil, his ideological offspring have adopted it with enthusiasm. The dictatorship of the proletariat is not, in the manner of Kautsky, reinterpreted to mean something positively innocuous; rather, it is simply and unequivocally renounced.[121]

The main architects of Eurocommunism were anxious to distinguish their ideas from 'lukewarm' social democracy. Their purpose, as defined by Carrillo, was 'to *transform* capitalist society, not to *administer* it'.[122] For Berlinguer, this

---

[117] 'The Skein of History Unrolled Backwards', in *Eurocommunism*, ed. G. R. Urban (London: Maurice Temple Smith, 1978), 81.
[118] *Eurocommunism and the State*, 100–1.
[119] Ibid. 12; *The Italian Road to Socialism*, 78.
[120] 'The Skein of History Unrolled Backwards', 77.
[121] See, e.g., Carrillo, *Eurocommunism and the State*, 154.
[122] Ibid. 104.

goal could be characterized as the 'progressive overcoming of the logic of capitalism'.[123] To be sure, they retained a residual attachment to Lenin. Listen again to Carrillo: 'Today when we read the polemics between Lenin and Kautsky . . . our approval goes without hesitation to Lenin's positions.' In backward Russia Leninist methods were 'an unavoidable historical necessity', and only a visitor from 'another planet' could seriously argue otherwise.[124] This ungracious attitude to Kautsky (arguably the first Eurocommunist) was surprisingly typical. Lucio Lombardo Radice probably spoke for most Italian communists when, in 1978, he praised Leninism to the hilt: 'Far from being a failure one would want to disown, it was and is the most powerful motor for liberation in human history.'[125] Sentimental hyperbole perhaps—but also indicative of a certain reluctance to let go of traditional symbols and verities. In truth, the Eurocommunists neither swore by nor abjured Lenin; they claimed that, true to his spirit, they were creatively applying Marxist ideas to particular historical conditions. In practice, this meant that they generally ignored him. According to Berlinguer and his like-minded colleagues, hardliners needed to be reminded that Lenin himself was unwilling 'to remain within the closed circle of old schemes and old formulae'.[126] It was the great man's doctrinal flexibility, as distinct from his substantive thoughts, that inspired his West European descendants.

It is doubtful whether we should still talk about Eurocommunism in the present tense. The term is no longer fashionable, and most of those who once embraced it have now forsaken it. The Italian comrades, submitting to the pitiless logic of changing circumstances, have even decided that they are not communists at all, and have changed their party label accordingly. After the upheavals of 1989–91, it is hard to present communism (Euro- or otherwise) as anything but a collection of outdated nostrums. At any rate, the Marxist credentials of Eurocommunism were always shaky. In its critique of capitalism—a system based 'on exploitation, on distor-

---

[123] *La proposta comunista*, 52.
[124] *Eurocommunism and the State*, 151–3.
[125] 'Communism with an Italian Face', in *Eurocommunism*, 47.
[126] Berlinguer, *La proposta comunista*, 101.

tion of consumption, on alienation', a system burdened by 'contradictions' and 'productive anarchy'—this reformed variant of communism did indeed assert its fidelity to classical Marxist texts.[127] Nor did it seek to deny that existing state forms are manipulated by monopoly capitalism in its own narrow interests. But, in concurring with Kautsky on the *essential* classlessness of liberal democracy, Carrillo, Berlinguer, *et al.* departed from both the spirit and letter of Marx's own position. Korsch repeatedly attacked Kautsky for his lack of 'creative, faithful revolutionary fantasy'.[128] Whatever one may think of the practicality of Korsch's own views, there is no disputing this assessment of his adversary. The 'human emancipation' exalted by Marx cannot be achieved through adherence to the values and practices of parliamentary democracy. This much was suggested in our previous chapter. It is now time to elaborate.

Commentators too easily dismiss Marxist rhetoric about liberal democracy being a creature of the bourgeoisie. Such rhetoric expresses two distinct propositions about the 'capitalist state': (a) that it exclusively serves the interests of some vaguely defined ruling class; and (b) that it reflects the individualistic values of those manufacturers and merchants who pioneered the development of capitalism—people commonly known as 'the rising bourgeoisie'. The first proposition, as we saw in Chapter 2, defies rational credence. But the second one would seem to contain a great deal of truth. Take the human rights or civil liberties normally associated with the liberal polity. These rights or freedoms are typically the basis of claims by individuals *against* the state or the wider community. To believe in them is to be committed to defending them, even when the universal interest may be harmed by doing so. Such rights need not be absolute (i.e. never vulnerable to legitimate infringement), but they must be seen as having a prima facie validity, which generally outweighs aggregative welfare considerations.[129] While respect for the rights of man may, as a rule, conduce to the collective good,

---

[127] Ibid. 7.

[128] *Karl Korsch: Revolutionary Theory*, 127.

[129] For an elaboration of this point, see J. L. Mackie, 'Can there be a Right-based Moral Theory?', in *Midwest Studies in Philosophy*, vol. iii, *Studies in*

what these rights evince, first and foremost, is the individual's desire not to be impinged upon, to be left alone, to enjoy a sphere of privacy sacred in itself. Freedom understood in this way is, as Isaiah Berlin notes, 'scarcely older, in its developed state, than the Renaissance or the Reformation'.[130] Like capitalism, it was a product of modernity, representing a mortal challenge to the holistic principles and arrangements of the old European order. The simultaneous ascent of the bourgeoisie and of natural rights doctrine could hardly have been accidental; Marx was correct to alert us to an intrinsic connection. Although it was absurd of him to confuse privacy with selfishness, and personal independence with human isolation, it was nevertheless true that the language of rights sprang from an individualistic, and much disputed, conception of human nature—a conception antithetical to Marx's own collectivism and historically linked to the needs and values of the bourgeoisie. One can reasonably call it 'bourgeois individualism', though (by underpinning rights) it surely benefits everyone. I am aware of the argument, advanced by many democratic socialists, that the greatest champion of civil liberties has been the organized working class, not the capitalists, who readily support authoritarian regimes when convenient. Maybe so, but this simply illustrates a point made by Marx: that the ideological weapons of the bourgeoisie can, in certain circumstances, be turned against it. In the final analysis, however, individual rights and all-encompassing communal solidarity are mutually antagonistic, as Marx himself realized. Rigorous and consistent enforcement of the former is compatible only with a modified (bourgeois?) form of socialism—one where there is no question, except *in extremis*, of sacrificing the individual's personal projects and vital interests to some unitary collective welfare.

Marx also criticized parliamentary government for detaching politics from the routines of everyday life. Apathy reigns supreme: citizens are passive spectators, content to leave public affairs to the experts. There is little reason to disagree with

Ethical Theory (1978), 356; and R. Dworkin, *Taking Rights Seriously* (London: Duckworth, 1977), 190–2.

[130] 'Two Concepts of Liberty', in *Four Essays on Liberty* (Oxford: Oxford University Press, 1969), 129.

this evaluation. Liberal democracy does rest on the assumption that people will defer to the wisdom of professional politicians and bureaucrats. The idea, dear to Marxist hearts, that men and women will find fulfilment only through active political participation is alien to the centripetal logic of parliamentarism—a logic very much evident in this century. And the less energy we devote to politics, the more energy we have to pursue our private ends, to cultivate our own gardens, to dedicate ourselves to the task of accumulation, which keeps the wheels of capitalism turning. Again, we see an affinity between liberal democracy and 'bourgeois individualism'.

Finally, we must ask if the Eurocommunist commitment to a pluralistic clash of opposing ideas and groups can be squared with Marxian collectivism. The Eurocommunists, in searching for a broad coalition to promote progressive change, have been forced to accept that social and cultural diversity is inherently valuable. But, at the end of the day, the 'politics of unity' is the politics of the lowest common denominator, inimical to the radical transformation of thought and behaviour that Marx envisaged. The endless haggling of an oriental bazaar was far from his ideal of human liberation. Recall, too, that Marx refused to acknowledge a symmetry between his own ideas (historical/scientific truth) and those of his opponents (ideological distortion). How could pluralism be desirable if it elevated falsehood to the same level as truth? Furthermore, Marx saw communism as a society without class antagonism; and since, from his materialist standpoint, political and cultural conflicts were merely disguised forms of class struggle, it followed that they would disappear along with the latter. In the realm of perfect unity, there would be no significant cleavages and hence no need for a multi-party system to express them. The people would speak with one voice—the voice of communism. *E pluribus unum* (out of many, one) may be the official motto of the United States, but it is more appropriate to the society Marx projected. For a consistent Marxist, the cacophony of pluralism is a bourgeois failing; something to be resisted, not glorified.

From both a theoretical and a practical point of view, the marriage between Marxism and liberal democracy has not been a success; in this sense Lenin was right and Kautsky wrong. But, upon seizing power, the Russian soon recognized the inadequacy of the participatory, or soviet, model as well. What was to be done? Building on Rousseau, he and later communists evolved what was in effect a third model of 'democracy', the vanguard model, which did at least manage to avoid the shortcomings (from a Marxist perspective) of the alternatives. But could it accurately be described as democratic?

IV   The Vanguard Model

Communist revolutionaries have faced a problem Marx himself did not fully appreciate: the inability of a majority whose attitudes have been 'warped' by a 'debased' society to realize in thought or deed their full human potential (as defined by Marxism). Long before the Russian Revolution, Lenin foresaw the difficulties ahead:

There is much talk of spontaneity. But the *spontaneous* development of the working-class movement leads to its subordination to bourgeois ideology, ... for the spontaneous working-class movement is trade-unionism ..., and trade-unionism means the ideological enslavement of the workers by the bourgeoisie.[131]

Whereas Marx and most classical Marxists saw the formation of socialist consciousness as an organic process, a natural product of the proletariat's experience of class struggle, the Bolsheviks concluded that people who had been deformed by capitalism could not be morally regenerated except by revolution, and that this required political power exercised by a vanguard, able to discern what needed to be done to save society. This argument expressed a paradox that has vexed all modern revolutionaries, starting with the French Jacobins, who decreed that ordinary citizens would have to be dragged, kicking and screaming if necessary, from the dark cave of the present into the dazzling sunlight of the future. What students of revolution term 'the paradox of emancipation' can be simply formulated: because the people have been subjected to comprehensive ideological manipulation, those who wish to liber-

[131] V. I. Lenin, *What is to be Done?* (Moscow: Progress Publishers, 1967), 41.

ate them must ignore their views. Freedom must be imposed, as it were, on the retarded masses. But why should rule by an enlightened vanguard be considered democratic? In answering this question, Lenin and his disciples made a unique contribution to Marxist theory.

Marxists of course see the community as a corporate entity, not as a random collection of autonomous individuals or groups. It is therefore possible (at least in the post-revolutionary society, where classes have been abolished) to define a unified popular consciousness that somehow transcends the actual thoughts of mere individuals. This idea harks back to Rousseau's much-discussed conception of the 'general will'. According to the great Swiss philosopher, diversity of opinion arises only when individuals lose sight of the public good and follow their own private interests. Thus Rousseau drew a distinction between the 'general will', always 'constant, unalterable and pure,' and the 'will of all', nothing more than a sum of 'particular', or selfish, wills.[132] The former exists whether people actually will it or not. It denotes what is true rather than what might, at any given moment, be empirically desired by the fallible majority. It is the 'real', *moral* will of the individual, in contrast to his or her arbitrary (selfish) will. Submission to the general will is therefore submission to one's 'higher self'. If an individual resists the general will, if his base self prevails over his higher self, then he may rightfully be compelled to comply with his better nature —'forced to be free', as Rousseau aptly put it.[133] Freedom and conformity converge in the selfless pursuit of the common good. In the Platonic mode, he equates the health of the body politic with flawless harmony:

the more concert reigns..., the nearer opinion approaches unanimity, the greater is the dominance of the general will. On the other hand, long debates, dissensions, and tumult proclaim the ascendancy of particular interests and the decline of the State.[134]

In spite of his aversion to 'long debates, dissensions, and tumult', Rousseau believed that direct democracy was the

---

[132] *The Social Contract*, 23, 86.
[133] Ibid. 15.
[134] Ibid. 87.

ideal mechanism for ascertaining the general will. Yet he was practical enough to recognize the 'paradox of emancipation' and the corresponding need for a 'superior intelligence', a divinely-inspired 'legislator', to guide people along the path of salvation:

> He who dares to undertake the making of a people's institutions ought to feel himself capable, so to speak, of changing human nature, of transforming each individual, who is by himself a complete and solitary whole, into part of a greater whole from which he in a manner receives his life and being.[135]

The 'legislator' is obviously a precursor of the vanguard party.

Like Rousseau (and notwithstanding his scientific pretensions) Lenin was essentially a moralist who sought to redeem men and women from their selfish follies and from the ill effects of their divisive social environment. This was of course a standard Marxist concern. What made Lenin original was his willingness to confront the élitist implications of Marxism's redemptive project. Until the creation of the new socialist man, most people cannot be trusted to renounce their own particular interests or seek the general will. To Lenin, even the industrial workers—history's chosen people—are under the sway of corrupt ideas. Left to their own devices, all they wish to do is wrangle over the price of their labour.[136] Members of *all* classes must, in consequence, be forcibly liberated from the tyranny of private passion and greed; they must be 'forced to be free'. The authentic (as opposed to the actual) will of the people is determined and expressed by the revolutionary vanguard, who embody Rousseau's 'superior intelligence'. In this Pickwickian sense, the people 'rule', though they may not know it.

But even if Marxism *is* truth, why should Lenin assume that it is the 'real' will of the people/workers? Lukács, in a helpful attempt to clarify the Leninist position, described class consciousness as 'the appropriate and rational reactions "imputed" [*zugerechnet*] to a particular typical position in the process of production. This consciousness is, therefore, neither the sum nor the average of what is thought or felt by the

---

[135] Ibid. 32.
[136] *What is to be Done?*, 31–41.

single individuals who make up the class.'[137] In other words, if the proletariat were perfectly 'rational', if they were not confused by capitalism's reifying tendencies, they would understand Marxism to be the world-view most 'appropriate' or natural to their material situation. Their 'empirically given' thoughts and feelings, on the other hand, are foisted upon them. Capitalism reduces them to ventriloquist's dummies, lacking a genuine voice of their own. Lukács has, I think, accurately rendered the thought processes of his Russian hero. But while Lenin certainly agreed that the workers' 'authentic' consciousness consisted of 'the thoughts and feelings appropriate to their objective situation',[138] we can perhaps convey the essential character of Leninist democracy without having recourse to metaphysical distinctions between real and actual wills. A more prosaic interpretation is possible. When describing the work of the soviets in 1919, Lenin remarked that they were 'in fact organs of government *for the working people* by the advanced section of the proletariat, but not by the working people as a whole'.[139] Bertrand Russell once observed that while the Western view of democracy 'is that it consists in the *rule* of the majority, the Russian view is that it consists in the *interests* of the majority'.[140] Not government *by* the people, but government *for* the people. Neither explicit nor implicit (i.e. 'real') consent is strictly required.

However we understand the vanguard conception of democracy (and the two interpretations outlined here are by no means mutually exclusive), the practical results would be the same. Lenin's cavalier approach to the mechanisms of popular participation first became evident in January 1918 when he dissolved the Constituent Assembly, because—to use his words—'the interests of the Revolution stand higher than the formal rights' of that body, within which the Bolsheviks were a minority party.[141] Transforming the once proud soviets into obedient instruments of Bolshevik rule was the next step in

[137] *History and Class Consciousness*, 51.
[138] Ibid.
[139] V. I. Lenin, 'Report on the Party Programme', 19 March 1919, in *Collected Works*, xxix, 183.
[140] *What is Democracy?* (London: Allen & Unwin, 1946), 14.
[141] V. I. Lenin, 'Theses on the Constituent Assembly', in *The Lenin Anthology*, ed. R. Tucker (New York: W. W. Norton, 1975), 421.

the consolidation of power. All of this was probably necessary to preserve the revolution in the face of civil war and capitalist encirclement. But Lenin made a virtue of necessity. What others saw as the suspension or abandonment of democracy was portrayed as a new and higher form of democracy—higher, that is, than 'venal and rotten parliamentarism'.[142]

Though Marx spoke of 'advanced and resolute' activists who would impart to the working class a scientific understanding of the historical process, he failed to notice the potential dangers (some would say the logical implications) of this pedagogic relationship. Intellectual élitism, in Marx, was tempered by a streak of populism. He never actually wanted the vanguard to pronounce itself the sole and final judge of proletarian interests. He never called for 'revolution from above'. Marx's more liberal-minded supporters repeatedly draw our attention to the famous passage where he was emphatic that 'the emancipation of the working classes must be conquered by the working classes themselves'.[143] Nor did he desire or envisage a post-revolutionary dictatorship by a minority, ruling in the name of the proletariat. All these innovations were the handiwork of Lenin, who made it clear, in both his writings and his actions, that participatory democracy was an ideal goal, not an immediate possibility. Even in *State and Revolution*, his most populist work, he praised the party as 'the vanguard of the proletariat, capable of assuming power and *leading the whole people* to socialism, of directing and organising the new system, of being the teacher, the guide, the leader of all the working and exploited people in organising their social life'.[144] The Bolsheviks did indeed assume power, teach the people, direct and organize the new system; and the result was, to Lenin, 'a million times more democratic than the most democratic bourgeois republic', because proletarian democracy is democracy 'for the vast majority of the population, for the exploited and for the toilers'.[145]

---

[142] *The State and Revolution*, 45.
[143] Passage from the General Rules Marx drafted for the International Working Men's Association, in K. Marx and F. Engels, *Selected Works*, ii (Moscow: Progress Publishers, 1976), 19.
[144] *The State and Revolution*, 25–6.
[145] *The Proletarian Revolution and the Renegade Kautsky*, 29–30.

Conceived in this way, democracy does not worship at the shrine of civil liberties or human rights, for it involves 'the necessary suppression of the exploiters', who must be 'crushed by force'.[146] Or—to adopt Rousseau's terminology—since the 'general will' is the 'real' will of every individual, there is no sense in the notion that individuals should be protected from it through constitutional limitations. To be sure, such checks and balances would be undemocratic, as they would hinder the implementation of the (implicit) popular mandate. Marx, too, opposed the imposition of constitutional restrictions on collective action. Lenin's novelty (and notoriety) resided in his assumption that the will of the people could be determined without the people having a say in the matter.

While Marx himself would almost certainly have recoiled from the vanguard model, he nevertheless laid its theoretical foundations. Two features of his thought are especially pertinent in this respect. The first is his interpretation of politics as little more than esoteric economics. If (as almost everyone agrees) democracy is about equal power, and if (as Marx said) the real source of power lies in the economic domain, then *genuine* democracy emerges only when disparities of economic power have been eliminated. Political arrangements are, strictly speaking, irrelevant. What counts is not *the way power is exercised*, but *who rules in the sphere of production*. Where liberal democratic procedures rest upon the concentration of property ownership, they merely confirm the wage slavery of the workers and the absolute dominion of capital. Where, on the other hand, dictatorial methods are necessary to guarantee the transfer of economic power into the hands of the masses, such methods may be called democratic. Lenin, by his own reckoning, was simply pursuing the logic of economic determinism when he made his apparently absurd statement that 'no essential contradiction can exist between the Soviet, that is, the socialist democracy, and the exercise of dictatorial power by a single person'.[147] 'Soviet democracy' is further underpinned by another axiom of Marxist determinism: the reduction of all systemic conflicts to class conflicts. Once

---

[146] *The State and Revolution*, 81–3.
[147] V. I. Lenin, 'The Immediate Tasks of the Soviet Government', Apr. 1918, *Collected Works*, xxvii, 268.

the means of production are taken into common ownership, classes (in the Marxist sense) cease to exist. There is no separate class of wealthy property owners, and no subservient class of wage slaves who own nothing but their labour power. In place of strife, there develops a homogeneity of interests throughout society. Since parties, in traditional Marxist analysis, always represent the antagonistic interests of different social classes, the case for a competitive or multiple party system disappears. A consensual popular will can effectively be expressed by a single, unchallenged party. As we saw, Kautsky offered sound reasons to reject this inference but, on this matter, as on many others, his was a voice in the wilderness. Even Togliatti thought that the ideal socialist democracy could dispense with a plurality of parties:

The dialectic of contradiction, which is essential for the development of society, no longer expresses itself in the competition between various parties . . . because there no longer exists either an objective basis (in things), or a subjective basis (in the minds of men) for such competition.[148]

Let us give the last word here to Stalin, who took credit for inventing the pleonastic term, 'people's democracy': 'The Constitution of the USSR is the only thoroughly democratic constitution in the world.' Why? As the toilers now own the means of production, and as there are 'no longer any antagonistic classes in society', party dictatorship ensures that 'the guidance of society . . . is in the hands of the working class'.[149] Cynical propaganda? One doubts it. For him, the happy conclusion (the USSR is 'thoroughly democratic') followed logically from Marxist premises.

The second feature of Marx's thought that lends support to the vanguard conception of democracy is his belief in a precise and empirically based science of human organization and progress, modelled on Newtonian physics. Just as the physical scientist searches for causal laws or invariant relationships, so Marx professed to lay bare the inexorable 'laws' which govern

[148] Interview with *Nuovi argomenti* (1956), in *On Gramsci and Other Writings*, 122.

[149] J. Stalin, 'On the Draft Constitution of the USSR', in *Problems of Leninism* (Moscow: Progress Publishers, 1945), 550, 557.

men and history with 'iron necessity', unaffected by individual human motives or intentions.[150] This claim underlies Lenin's view (only implicit in Marx himself) that the vanguard could postulate the workers' 'objective' interests without actually testing their opinion. After all, the validity of a scientific theory is independent of how many people happen to accept it. Herein lies the source of the utter certitude (moral and political) that actuates communists and infuriates their opponents. Yet at first glance Marxism might seem to be the least dogmatic of world-views. Communists, Marx once boasted, 'do not preach morality at all'. Certainly, the doctrine does seem to embody a kind of relativism, at least with respect to normative questions. When Lenin asserted that there was in Marxism 'not a grain of ethics from beginning to end',[151] when Trotsky dismissed moral ideals as 'fetishes', 'philosphic gendarmes of the ruling class',[152] they did no more than echo Marx's own loathing of ethical appeals and affirm their faith in the central tenet of historical materialism: that, as Marx put it, 'the phantoms formed in the human brain' are 'necessary sublimations of man's material life process', mere products of underlying pressures and circumstances.[153] Thus values, be they moral or political, are not fixed stars in some Platonic firmament, eternal, immutable, identical for all men and women. The belief in ethereal, crystalline ethical laws, transcending material reality, is mythological, of religious origin. So said the Marxists. Historical materialism brings morality down to earth from these celestial heights: we discover its

[150] See prefaces to the first and second editions of his master-work, *Capital*, in *Marx & Engels: Basic Writings*, 133–7 and 143–5. These prefaces, where Marx likens himself to a physicist and describes the evolution of society as 'a process of natural history', are invaluable sources for those who wish to unearth his intentions and self-image. Whether Marx was—even in his later years—entirely consistent in his scientific determinism is of course another matter. Many Marxists, notably Lukács and Gramsci, have fought a rearguard action against those who would equate Marxism with positivistic science.

[151] Quoted in S. Lukes, *Marxism and Morality* (Oxford: Clarendon Press, 1985), 21.

[152] L. Trotsky, 'Their Morals and Ours' (a pamphlet published in 1938), reproduced in *Their Morals and Ours: Marxist versus Liberal Views on Morality*, four essays by L. Trotsky, J. Dewey, and G. Novack, 4th edn. (New York: Pathfinder Press, 1969), 36–7.

[153] *The German Ideology*, in *Writings of the Young Marx*, 415.

roots in class struggle and, ultimately, in the forward progress of technical innovation.

But this demystification of human values poses a problem. If Marxism is concerned only with 'recognition of the necessary', if it eschews intoxication with trans-historical moral ideals, if it frowns upon ethical speculation and denies the existence of independent rational standards, valid for all time and for all peoples, then how can it issue imperatives about human behaviour or condemn the inequities of capitalism? How can it avoid the 'epistemological defeatism' that would appear to follow logically from the necessarily class-determined character of all thought? The answer lies in the historical dialectic. Despite their contextual understanding of morality, the classical Marxists were anything but relativists. History, in their eyes, carried its own objective recommendations, showed the progressive solution of tasks, and thus united 'what is' and 'what ought to be'. Communism was inscribed in the historical process; it was an objective necessity, guaranteed by the dynamics of capitalism, and as such it represented unquestionable truth about how we should live. Marx and his disciples refused to draw a rigid dividing line between 'fact' and 'value'. In their opinion, ethical imperatives could be reduced, without residue, to descriptive propositions. It was therefore possible to derive moral concepts from the material conditions of life, or, more specifically, from the findings of empirical science. The Marxist scientists, then, set themselves up as arbiters of 'objective truth'[154]—not only about how we *do* actually behave but also about how we *ought* to behave. According to their own self-image, they were in a position to supply final solutions to what J. S. Mill called 'the greatest questions which can occupy humanity'.[155] Whatever surface appearances may suggest, mainstream Marxism

---

[154] G. Plekhanov, *The Development of the Monist View of History* (Moscow: Progress Publishers, 1956), 195 (the book was first published in 1895). He adds that henceforth all the new discoveries of human thought 'will supplement and confirm the theory of Marx, just as new discoveries have supplemented and confirmed the discovery of Copernicus'. This identification of Marxism with scientific truth was accepted as gospel by a whole generation of Marxists, for whom Plekhanov may stand as a prime example.

[155] 'On Liberty', in *Utilitarianism, Liberty, and Representative Government* (London: Dent, 1910), 94.

never, in actual fact, wished to dispense with moral judgements; it sought, rather, to give them the objectivity of scientific description.

Captivated by this view of morality as a science, with 'right' and 'wrong' answers, Lenin, by the turn of the century, began to wonder aloud why revolutionaries should pay heed to the spontaneous perceptions and beliefs of ordinary people. Given the assumptions he shared with his fellow Marxists, he had a valid point. On a passenger airliner, to take an obvious example, no one would dream of arguing that the pilot should submit navigational questions to the democratic scrutiny of the passengers, for these are technical concerns, to be dealt with by those who have, through intense study, acquired the appropriate knowledge. Would non-engineers presume to participate in decisions as to how best to construct a bridge? Long before Lenin, Plato sagely drew the inference that where absolute truths are comprehended by a few, there is no need of public deliberation. Leninism is a lineal descendant of Platonism. It is up to the revolutionary scientists (Guardians) to discover our 'real' interests—and hence our 'real' will. The new society is to be guided by knowledge, not by mass preferences and volitions. Those who hold 'incorrect' ethical or political views are no more worthy of serious consideration than the crackpot who insists on the earth's flatness. To quote the hero of 1917:

The modern use of the term 'freedom of criticism' contains... inherent falsehood. Those who are really convinced that they have made progress in science would not demand freedom for the new views to continue side by side with the old, but the substitution of the new views for the old.[156]

The staples of liberal democracy—competitive elections, majority rule, freedom of expression—would seem to serve little purpose if the monolithic general will, or the people's interests, can be objectively defined by a scientific élite, ordained by 'History'. The identification of socialist democracy with the pursuit of these interests, the implementation of this will, is an intelligible, if not a necessary, conclusion to draw.

[156] Lenin, *What is to be Done?*, 11.

When socialist states describe (or should we say described) themselves as 'people's democracies' they are/were referring, at bottom, to this vanguard model of democracy. 'People's democracy' is a relatively recent addition to the Marxist lexicon, having been coined in the aftermath of the Second World War. The label applied specifically to the new satellite states of Eastern Europe, or to forms of government which imitated the Soviet system, not to the Soviet system itself. This is because its declared role as 'guiding state' did not permit an identity with the 'guided states'. But since communist literature has adopted the expression 'people's democracy' without recalling such distinctions, and since, even in the original usage, these regimes were mere copies (in the Platonic sense) of the 'idea' realized in Soviet democracy, we can extend the term to cover the USSR. From the operational point of view, the differences between the satellite 'democracies' and their Soviet paragon were barely appreciable. The only dissimilarity worth mentioning was more apparent than real. In contrast to the formal monism of the Soviet Union, which was (until 1990) enshrined in the Constitution,[157] other people's democracies maintained a nominal pluralism of political parties (though the only parties tolerated were those that accepted communist hegemony). The reasons for the preservation of a multiple party system were purely tactical. After the war, communists were anxious to enlist the support of a wide range of political forces in the newly liberated lands. In part this policy reflected a recognition of Marxism's shallow roots in the societies of East–Central Europe; in part it was a matter of 'window-dressing for foreign consumption'.[158] But no serious attempt was made to hide the fact that this selec-

---

[157] See Article 6 of the *Constitution (Fundamental Law) of the Union of Soviet Socialist Republics*, adopted in 1977 (Moscow: Novosti Press, 1977), 21. The Article reads as follows: 'The leading and guiding force of Soviet society and the nucleus of its political system, of all state organisations and public organisations, is the Communist Party of the Soviet Union. The CPSU exists for the people and serves the people. The Communist Party, armed with Marxism-Leninism, determines the general perspectives of the development of society and the course of the home and foreign policy of the USSR, directs the great constructive work of the Soviet people, and imparts a planned, systematic and theoretically substantiated character to their struggle for the victory of communism.'

[158] F. J. Kase, *People's Democracy* (Leiden: A. W. Sijthoff, 1968), 96.

tive political pluralism was temporary, destined sooner or later to give way to the higher political truth of a one-party system.[159] And, regardless of the actual constitutional provisions and techniques, the communist oligarchy was, for all practical purposes, the real and exclusive power-holder. Even when the monopoly of power was exercised through a nominal coalition with other parties, their subservience was usually assured by the endorsement of a common programme prepared in detail by the communist bosses.[160] The *locus potestatis* was always the Communist Party or, more accurately, a small oligarchy within that party. A uniform pattern of political rule took hold throughout the communist world. People's democracy, whatever its specific form, was not a method for implementing the people's expressed or explicit wishes; it was, on the contrary, a state with a clearly defined purpose— building socialism—which it would pursue *regardless* of the actual will of the people.

Recall, however, that the vanguard model of democracy (on one interpretation at any rate) presupposes a dichotomy between 'real' and empirically discernible wills. In all people's democratic constitutions, it is claimed that political power emanates from the people, and that this is precisely what people's democracy means. In the words of N. P. Farberov, once regarded as the USSR's premier expert in public law, 'the people's character of the people's democratic state is determined solely by the fact that the political power is in the hands of the toilers led by the communist party'.[161] But this attribution of power, far from implying that the political

---

[159] H. G. Skilling , ' "People's Democracy" in Soviet Theory—II', *Soviet Studies*, 3: 2 (1951), 146.

[160] This does not necessarily mean that the subordinate parties were bereft of influence. According to Jerzy Wiatr and Adam Przeworski, we should not overlook the subtle pressures exercised behind the scenes through delicate negotiations and bargaining: 'The allied parties do not compete for power but present their candidates jointly with the hegemonic party. They do not challenge its leadership in those fields which are vital for the state. But they are officially recognized as representatives of selected sectors of the population such as the peasants, craftsmen, etc. and they are consulted whenever a decision concerns issues of vital interest for the groups they are supposed to represent.' See 'Control Without Opposition', *Government and Opposition*, 1 (1965–6), 237.

[161] Quoted in Kase, *People's Democracy*, 90–1.

leaders simply carry out the opinions of the 'toilers', is a logical derivation from Marxist-Leninist axioms. In determining the essence of the state, the decisive aspect is not the mere form of political organization, but the economic content which comprises the flesh and blood of the organization. And the economic content of people's democracy is public (people's) ownership of the means of production. Because the toilers (supposedly) enjoy economic power, the political regime automatically fulfils their objective interests, and hence their 'real will'. Strictly speaking, this will could be expressed through the dictatorial power of a single party or even (as Lenin suggested) a single person. Yet the people's democratic constitutions did contain a variety of mechanisms and forms through which citizens could, to all appearances, make their voices heard. Communist regimes have always been reluctant to abandon the customary trappings of democracy, if only for reasons of propaganda. Although the vanguard model finds sustenance in important aspects of Marx's thinking, it by no means accords with his preferred principles of political organization. Communist leaders could not simply ignore the lofty Marxian goal of workers ruling themselves through mass participation in the daily business of politics. Channels for citizen 'participation' were duly provided. While the various countries differed in detail, certain practices were common to all of them.

Participation in communist systems has taken two forms: (i) direct involvement, both official and unofficial; and (ii) voting in elections. Communist apologists have always been keen to point out that 'representative authorities do not exhaust the forms of influence of the people over the exercise of state power'.[162] The ruling ideology laid it down that mass participation was direct as well as indirect, thereby giving the regimes 'a special, popular character'.[163] There was some truth in this claim. All over the Soviet Union and Eastern Europe, officially recognized village and block meetings allowed ordinary citizens to express opinions regarding the efficiency

[162] W. Zakrzewski, 'The Mechanism of Popular Activity in the Exercise of State Authority in People's Poland', in *Representation*, ed. J. R. Pennock and J. W. Chapman (New York: Atherton Press, 1968), 275.

[163] Ibid. 260.

of local administration. Such gatherings could discuss (and presumably influence) the maintenance of buildings, streets, and open spaces. In addition, workers' councils, with varying degrees of power, were institutionalized in most communist regimes. Only in Yugoslavia, though, were the principles of worker autonomy taken at all seriously. Within specified boundaries, councils could hire and fire managers and generally perform entrepreneurial functions: pricing, marketing, the disposal of capital funds. Given its extensive emloyment of market mechanisms, however, Yugoslavia was unique in the communist bloc. In other regimes, labouring under 'the dictatorship of the plan', the councils were purely advisory.[164] Communist systems have also, in the post-Stalin years, made considerable use of public meetings to discuss forthcoming legislation. Prior to the passage of a pensions act in the USSR, for instance, such preliminary deliberations gave rise to more than 13,000 suggestions from members of the public.[165] In general, ruling communist parties sought out citizen complaints, suggestions, and recommendations—so long as these did not challenge official policies. Even during the Brezhnev era, all of the media chiefs in the Soviet Union, including editorial boards of broadcasting stations, not only published but positively encouraged letters from the public. Where appropriate, communications were forwarded to relevant government agencies, who often acted upon the contents.

For all their emphasis on active, direct involvement, the people's democracies took special pains to mimic parliamentary *procedures*, while simultaneously mocking parliamentary (i.e. liberal) *values*. Elections to legislatures were used by reigning communist parties as nationwide plebiscites for the endorsement of official programmes and policies. Elections were never used to oppose the communist oligarchy, and, until the 1980s, rarely used as contests for office between candidates. The widely adopted Soviet format was for the overwhelming majority of voters to elect the officially supported list, containing one candidate per seat. The usual choice open to the individual voter was to vote either for or against

---

[164] For a useful discussion of the situation up to 1973, see R. C. Gripp, *The Political System of Communism* (London: Nelson, 1973), 123–6.
[165] Ibid. 112.

this one list. Only tiny minorities, sometimes less than one per cent, ever summoned up the courage to vote against.[166] Before the revolutionary changes of the Gorbachev era, which formally jettisoned anything akin to communism, the USSR did not deviate from this curious electoral pattern. Soviet-type elections have been amusingly described as 'choice Paradise-style': as God said to Adam, 'Here is Eve, the woman of your choice.'[167] By and large, the East European satellite states offered their citizens a greater selection of candidates. The situation varied from one country to another; but by the mid-1980s, it was common for electoral laws to require that the number of candidates exceed the number of positions to be filled. With few exceptions, however, all candidates had to be approved by the communist authorities, and the top national leaders had reserved places in the parliament or else enjoyed the privilege of standing unopposed. Multi-candidate elections furnished no institutionalized means by which the mass public could change the direction of national policy.[168]

Given the manner of their recruitment, communist legis-latures have been dismissed as rubber-stamp bodies, simple instruments for the quick and automatic ratification of party policies. True, neither vigorous dissension nor organized opposition was ever much in evidence. But by the late 1950s, these legislatures began to acquire more and more influence as articulators of popular demands and grievances. In par-ticular, the Polish *Sejm* and Yugoslavia's *Skupcina* asserted themselves with some frequency, occasionally forcing govern-ments to amend their party-approved proposals.[169] Still, unquestioned communist hegemony made fundamental opposition to the party programme unthinkable. In the final analysis, communist elections were, as Michael Waller

[166] In the Supreme Soviet election of 1937, Stalin received more than 100% of the potential vote, it being explained later that voters in neighbour-ing constitutencies had insisted on casting their vote in the Moscow district where he had been standing. See S. White, 'Reforming the Electoral System', *The Journal of Communist Studies*, 4 (Dec. 1988), 3.

[167] O. Ulc, 'Legislative Politics in Czechoslovakia', in *Communist Legisla-tures in Comparative Perspective*, ed. D. Nelson and S. White (Albany: SUNY Press, 1982), 116.

[168] W. G. Hahn, 'Electoral "Choice" in the Soviet Bloc', *Problems of Communism*, 36 (March/Apr. 1987), 29–39.

[169] Gripp, *The Political System of Communism*, 116.

wrote in 1981, 'purely confirmatory; they in fact reinforce verticality'.[170] They had no effect whatsoever on the crucial question of 'who shall govern', and their effect on policies was minimal to non-existent. Indeed, to apply the label 'election' to these humiliating spectacles required 'an unacceptable semantic stretching of the term "election"'.[171] Leonard Schapiro, in one of his magisterial studies of Soviet politics, concluded that a communist 'election' served three main purposes. First, it provided 'a public demonstration of the legitimacy of the regime'. Secondly, it was 'an invaluable educational and propaganda exercise', affording a golden opportunity to stress the wisdom and achievements of the Party and to disseminate its promises for an even more glorious future. Thirdly, it supplied proof that 'the system of control is unimpaired'.[172] Whereas elections, as normally understood, are designed to ensure government from below, communist elections functioned to reinforce 'government from the top'.[173] It is one of history's little ironies that the people who mounted and defended these pseudo-events were the very same people who denounced Western elections as 'purely formal'. To rephrase an old adage, the pot cannot hide its own true colour by calling the kettle black.

The communist demand for at least the outward appearance of popular control clearly signalled something new in the history of dictatorship. Unsympathetic commentators, such as Schapiro, noted that the typical communist regime was not merely an authoritarian government, a small élite group lording it over a static traditional society. Instead, it was a dynamic totalitarian system, which set as its ideal the active involvement of all citizens in the affairs of a rapidly developing society. What was required, however, was not participation in the *formulation* of public policy but in its *execution* and *celebration*. In short, participation in communist systems was, and remains, a cynical charade. This view has not gone

[170] *Democratic Centralism* (Manchester: Manchester University Press, 1981), 76.
[171] Ibid. 80.
[172] *The Government and Politics of the Soviet Union* (London: Hutchinson, 1967), 108.
[173] Ibid. 143.

unchallenged, even in the West. Some commentators have advanced a more favourable interpretation, highlighting the gradual increase in consultation and freedom of expression after Stalin's demise. While these trends were visible all over Eastern Europe, the debate focused on the USSR. Jerry Hough, in an important article published in 1976, put forward the claim that the mechanisms of participation, including elections, furnished Soviet policy-makers with significant 'feedback information', enabling them to respond to drifts in the moods and concerns of the public. At the level of particulars, 'citizen input' had an impact on policy outcomes. He concluded that the familiar paradigm of the USSR as a 'directed society' was misleading.[174] T. H. Rigby, in a rejoinder to Hough's argument, reminded us that although Soviet citizens could contribute to the implementation of official policies and influence local decisions within the framework of those policies, they could not actively oppose those policies or attack the leaders who formulated them, or work openly for alternatives: '... public participation is limited to dotting i's and crossing t's or at best contributing marginally to the climate of opinion in which later choices may be made'.[175]

Though these issues no longer have any currency, it is always useful to set the historical record straight. The present writer pretends to no special expertise in Soviet or communist politics, but it is worth observing that the aforementioned arguments, while differing in tone and emphasis, are actually complementary. Party bosses no doubt saw participation as a tool of propaganda and mobilization; on the other hand, they probably placed a great deal of value on 'feedback' from the citizenry. Such input would be practically helpful to the central planners, as it would serve to identify particular shortages and inefficiencies. Meanwhile, responding to it would nourish communist leaders in their (apparent) belief that they enjoyed a spiritual communion with the masses. There is no need to assume that these leaders were *either* manipulative *or* idealistic in their approach to participation. They may well have

---

[174] 'Political Participation in the Soviet Union', *Soviet Studies*, 28 (Jan. 1976), 15–17.

[175] 'Hough on Political Participation in the Soviet Union', *Soviet Studies*, 28 (Apr. 1976), 260.

been both, for human motives are rarely clear-cut. What is
more, Marxist doctrine offered no coherent guidance on this
question. The schizophrenia of communist political practice
(democratic forms and dictatorial substance) reflected the
schizophrenia of Marxism itself: the people must rule, but
only if and when they can demonstrate a grasp of higher
dialectical reality. Seen in this light, communist ambival-
ance towards popular participation becomes wholly
comprehensible.

The ambivalence is strikingly exemplified by Arthur Kiss, a
distinguished Hungarian academician, whose book *Marxism
and Democracy* presents a lengthy and relatively sophisticated
defence of 'people's democracy'. This, he assures us, is 'majority democracy both in its *content* and in the *mode of exercising* power'.[176] It is 'the only system in world history' where
ordinary people enjoy 'real power', where 'the government
and masses are in unity'.[177] Communist leaders are '*the delegates of the people and are accountable to the people for their
activity*'.[178] Indeed: 'The Marxist-Leninist party is the supreme
instrument of the realization, formulation and assertion of
the will and interests of the working masses.'[179] One might
therefore suppose that the overwhelming majority support the
party. Well, not necessarily. Kiss admits that the empirical
'majority' in 'numerous socialist countries' might, if given the
choice, prefer a 'petty bourgeois' form of rule. But any such
deviation should be resisted, as it 'runs counter to the fundamental interests of socialism and of the workers'.[180] Anti-
socialist forces—the objective enemies of the people—must
be repelled with 'adequate weaponry'.[181] In 'numerous socialist countries', he concludes, there are phases when the party
rules 'in the name of the people' and without their explicit
consent, simply because the people fail to perceive their 'genuine aspirations'. Lamenting this popular deficiency, he declares, as if it were self-evident, 'that the principle of mass

---

[176] *Marxism and Democracy* (Budapest: Akadémiai Kiado, 1982), 160.
[177] Ibid. 31, 216.
[178] Ibid. 312.
[179] Ibid. 293.
[180] Ibid. 294.
[181] Ibid. 260.

democracy is incompatible with the revolutionary vanguard being led by the given intellectual state or by the mood of the masses'.[182] But in no way does this 'rule from above' undermine 'genuine people's sovereignty' in socialist society.[183] For the *real* will of the people—or else the actual will of the real people ('the *genuine* majority')—is incarnated in the vanguard party.[184]

Our brief analysis of Kiss's argument underlines how misleading it is for Western observers, like Michael Levin, to talk about the 'wide gulf' between communist ideology and practice.[185] For the vanguard model of democracy is clearly an explicit and integral part of communist ideology. What we *can* say (and Kiss makes this apparent) is that Marxist-Leninist doctrine is fundamentally inconsistent in its demand for both political control from above and popular initiative from below. This confusion, moreover, mirrors the contradictions within Marx's own thought. The problem is not that communist leaders cynically discarded their ideological commitments; it is that these commitments simultaneously pulled them in opposite directions. Painful awareness of this dilemma led to the invention of that infamous oxymoron, 'democratic centralism'—Lenin's bewildering contribution to the Marxist dictionary.[186]

[182]   Ibid. 217, 247.
[183]   Ibid. 206.
[184]   Ibid. 148 (my emphasis).
[185]   *Marx, Engels and Liberal Democracy*, 164.
[186]   Lenin begot the term in 1906 and intended it to be the guiding organizational principle of the revolutionary party. But after the October revolution brought about the fusion of party and state, 'democratic centralism' eventually came to be interpreted as a constitutional principle at the level of the state. By 'democratic' Lenin meant that the elected Party Congress was to be supreme over policy. By 'centralism' he meant that once general policy was agreed, the everyday decisions of the central bodies were absolutely binding on all members, who were expected to march in step, whatever their private reservations. This supposed synthesis of procedural democracy and central control represented a departure from Lenin's earlier (pre-1906) thinking, not to mention his later practice, in which the 'command' element was uppermost. Once in power, the Bolsheviks found that disciplined centralization, with its requirement of unanimity, was antithetical to free democratic debate, either within the party or within society at large. To insist on monolithic unity in the implementation of policy is to discourage, if not destroy, those regions of nonconformity within which alternative viewpoints can flourish. See Waller, *Democratic Centralism*, for an excellent analysis (historical and conceptual) of this odd concept.

The task now stands before us of answering the question whether a vanguard state can properly be considered democratic. It might seem otiose to quarrel about political labels, as the meanings given to them rarely admit of final stipulation. Is it really possible to discover a 'true' definition of democracy, one that would enable us to separate the democratic sheep from the pseudo-democratic goats? Beyond a certain point, no. While, at a very high level of abstraction, contested concepts such as 'freedom' or 'democracy' might be said to have a peculiar and indisputable essence, their application to the real world will always be a matter of selective judgement rather than deductive logic. Disputes over usage are both inevitable and (if they should help us to clarify our own ideas) fruitful. Still, words are instruments of communication, necessarily bounded by their linguistic and historical connotations. Furthermore, words have consequences: to name a thing in a certain way is the same as to determine in advance how that thing should be interpreted. Since words convey thought, their blatant misuse can corrupt and distort it. And once we stop caring about the meaning of democracy, we may stop caring about the thing itself. It is therefore dangerous to undervalue the terminological element of political debate. When words are used in eccentric or inconsistent ways, political analysts are obliged to expose these linguistic misdeeds. Having said this, we must also grant that the term 'democracy' is ambiguous in the extreme. Etymologically, it undoubtedly began as the name for a form of rule, 'rule by the people', as contrasted with 'aristocracy' or 'oligarchy' (rule by the few), and with 'monarchy' (rule by one person). But the word democracy has also been associated with a set of ideals, equality in particular. In ordinary usage, when we refer to an institution—say, Oxford University or the British Civil Service—as 'undemocratic', we often mean that it is unequalitarian in its composition or criteria of entry. C. B. Macpherson defends the democratic credentials of communist states by drawing attention to this dual meaning. He distinguishes between 'the narrow or strict sense' and the 'broader sense' of democracy. In the former sense, it is a system of government where the people, or at least the majority, control those who make and enforce political decisions. On this definition, the vanguard model is democratic only if we accept the mystical division between 'actual' and 'real' wills. If, on the other hand, the broader concept of democracy as equality is allowed, the claims of the communist vanguard state appear legitimate, since its final aim is human equality. While this may not be government *by* the people, it is, arguably, government *for* the people.[187]

According to Jack Lively, Macpherson rests his argument on a fundamental misconception about traditional usage. For democracy in the *political* context has normally referred to equality of power over decision-making. It has been assumed, historically, that political equality would ineluctably bring social equality; but no one before Lenin, not even the ancient Greeks, *equated* political democracy with social levelling.[188] To adapt President Lincoln's ringing phrase, democracy *means* government *by* the people; whether this results in government *for* the people is, *pace* Lincoln, an empirical question. The people, after all, are often muddled in their thinking, and perhaps they are frequently mistaken about the best ways of achieving either their desired goals on their full potential as human beings. We can envisage situations where an inexperienced or illiterate population, burdened by what Marx called 'the muck of Ages', would be well advised to submit to an élite of enlightened experts. Still, benevolent despotism does not equal democracy.

There may, however, be another way of defending the democratic claims of the vanguard state. In terms of strict logic, it is possible for an élite or even an individual to embody the prevailing opinions of the larger community. It may well be, for example, that Stalin (or Hitler for that matter) accurately reflected the actual wishes of his people, despite the obvious rigging of elections (plebiscites in Nazi Germany). Traditionally, political democracy has not been associated with individual rights and humanitarian behaviour; it has simply denoted popular rule, and this can plausibly be interpreted as implementation of the majority's known preferences, however authoritarian or coercive the regime might be. Jane Mansbridge has argued that where there is overwhelming agreement on political objectives democracy does not require

---

[187] *The Real World of Democracy* (New York: Oxford University Press, 1972), 18–22.
[188] *Democracy* (Oxford: Basil Blackwell, 1975), 34–5.

equality of power or formal mechanisms of consultation. She urges us to recognize a distinction between 'unitary' democracy and 'adversary' democracy. The latter, we are informed, is the conventional understanding of democracy as a fair method for weighing up conflicting interests. By instituting the formal procedures of 'one citizen, one vote' and majority rule, this form of democracy aims for an equal distribution of power. But, according to Mansbridge, this adversarial process violates 'another, older understanding of democracy', based on consensus and common interest as opposed to conflict and self-aggrandizement. This is unitary democracy, whose ideal is (to borrow the Greek word) *homonoia*, unanimity, being 'of one mind'.[189] And 'where interests are identical, equal power is irrelevant'.[190] One group of people—'the oldest members, the intellectual vanguard, the most interested, or the best administrators'—can wield more power than the others and still exercise that power with the consent of all.[191] She is careful to observe that the unitary conception is most appropriate in a society or association that is both small in size (thus allowing for face-to-face relationships and constant exchange of information) and rudimentary in its division of labour (thus ensuring similarity of perspective and interest). As the modern nation-state does not meet these conditions, the unitary ideal has been relegated to the margins of political discourse and practice. Yet this solidaristic type of democracy —or something approximating it—lives on in, for example, hippie communes, worker co-operatives, and New England town meetings.

Mansbridge's attempt to divorce political democracy from equal power is questionable on grounds of common usage. It might be contended that her argument relies upon an unwarranted conflation of power and authority. But let us, in order to construct the best possible case for the Leninist brethren, assume that she is right. If we could further accept the idea of an entire nation being 'of one mind', we could possibly view communist vanguard states as unitary democracies, where

---

[189] *Beyond Adversary Democracy* (Chicago: University of Chicago Press, 1983), 3.
[190] Ibid. 19.
[191] Ibid. 30.

the monolithic national consensus finds expression through a wise élite, perfectly in touch with the people's wishes. It is inconceivable, however, that the citizens of a complex, large-scale society would approach unanimity on all issues; and even if they did, the rulers would have no way of knowing this in the absence of adversarial procedures, which are specifically designed for the purpose of eliciting and testing opinion in societies where distances and sheer numbers limit the possibilities of face-to-face discussion. Opinion surveys, usually based on leading or ambiguous questions, and conducted in a void where choices are without consequences, offer no effective substitute for free elections. In vast, impersonal societies, moreover, a fair electoral procedure presupposes a framework of civil liberties: freedom of association and assembly plus free access to various communication and publicity media, along with the right to criticize and dissent. Where such liberties are missing, where there are no free and competitive elections, it can be plausibly assumed that what passes for consensus is the product of fear, ignorance, and/or manipulation. Any claim on the part of the regime to embody the people's unified will (actual or 'real') could therefore be dismissed as so much hot air. Even the more modest claim to represent a majority would scarcely be credible. In countries where the voters are allowed to express approval or disapproval of governmental policies, both the majority and the minority are fluid. The majority, that is to say, is a variable entity: on different issues it will consist of different people. Whether an election is won by candidate X or candidate Y will often depend on which issues have become most prominent during the campaign. Equally pertinent, people's opinions will change rapidly in light of new circumstances or new information or new arguments. The upshot is that no government can justifiably assert that it has a *permanent* majority of the people behind it. Public support must be determined through the frequent application of adversarial principles.

'People's democracy' was nothing more than a metaphysical notion, an article of dogma never verified by accepted procedural methods. It was a kind of pseudo-democracy in which rituals associated with the democratic idea were preserved on the surface but given an authoritarian content. The unreality of communist pretensions was dramatically exposed in 1989 and again in 1991, when the 'people' in question delivered their collective verdict on the unique brand of 'democracy' that had been imposed on them. *Homonoia*, unanimity, finally made its presence felt, to the horror of its erstwhile champions. In an ironic twist of the historical dialectic, the vanguard model of democracy was consigned to Engels's 'museum of antiquities'.

V Concluding Remarks

We must conclude that Marxism has failed to produce a coherent and convincing theory of democracy. Marx himself, though writing little of substance on the subject, clearly hoped for some species of participatory democracy, unencumbered by 'parasitic' politicians and bureaucrats. But this hope sat uneasily alongside his preference for a centrally regulated, large-scale industrial economy. Later Marxists, acknowledging the impossibility of reconciling the irreconcilable, chose to rediscover the virtues of the liberal political system, whose structure appeared compatible with the realities of socialist production. But it was always quixotic to attempt to graft liberal principles on to an intrinsically anti-liberal philosophy. A protected private sphere, personal independence, unrestricted diversity of opinion and behaviour—these cherished liberal values were precisely what Marx and his votaries denigrated in their quest for an organic society. Lenin, while agreeing that liberal democracy was an odious insult to mankind, was less than sanguine about the immediate prospects for a participatory society of the sort envisaged by radical Marxists. Accordingly, he and his successors developed a vanguard conception of democracy. Close inspection, however, reveals this to be a travesty, negating everything that genuine democrats stand for. The Leninists implicitly (and perhaps unconsciously) conceded this unpleasant fact by dressing up their despotic regimes in traditional democratic garb: elections, representative assemblies, mass meetings; but the inner reality remained imperfectly concealed by these outer garments. In practice, Marxism has achieved nothing better than vanguard dictatorship, differing from one country to another only in its degree of brutality and cynicism. Was this sorry state of affairs inevitable? Or was it based on a faulty understanding or even deliberate distortion of Marx's own writings? We now turn to a systematic examination of these issues.

4 Marxism and Despotism

> [T]he course taken by history holds nasty surprises, and is ruled...not so much by the cunning of reason which guarantees that bad causes have a good outcome, as by the malice of unreason which perverts even the most well-intentioned acts.
>
> NORBERTO BOBBIO, *Which Socialism?*

'HISTORY is merciless to all ideologies.'[1] So writes Ferenc Feher, lamenting how the Marxian dream of emancipation turned into a nightmare of authoritarian collectivism. Why have Marxist states failed so miserably in their task of building the 'realm of freedom'? Why is it that Marxism, a doctrine devoted to human liberation, has repeatedly inspired the creation of despotic regimes? In reply, some Marxists simply deny the validity of the question. For them, existing or past communist regimes tell us no more about the essence of Marxism 'than the reign of a Borgia Pope does about the essence of Christianity'.[2] According to Keith Graham, for example, Marxism, properly understood, 'is the antithesis of the one-party states and bureaucratic élites taking Marx's name'.[3] Similarly, Jean Elleinstein, an influential member of the French Communist Party, complains: 'What has happened to Marxism in Russian hands...was a deviation from Marx's thinking and, in extreme cases, a denial and repudiation of Marxism.'[4] The assumption underlying this statement, that the practical application of a set of ideas discloses nothing about the nature of those ideas, is an odd one for a Marxist to make, since it

---

[1] 'The Dictatorship over Needs', *Telos*, 35 (Spring 1978), 31.
[2] K. Graham, *The Battle of Democracy: Conflict, Consensus and the Individual* (Brighton: Wheatsheaf Books, 1986), 170.
[3] Ibid. 202.
[4] 'The Skein of History Unrolled Backwards', in *Eurocommunism*, ed. G. R. Urban (London: Maurice Temple Smith, 1978), 85.

was Marx's plain intention to unite theory and practice. As he said in his second Thesis on Feuerbach, 'The question whether human thinking can reach objective truth—is not a question of theory but a *practical* question. In practice man must prove the truth, that is, actuality and power, . . . of his thinking.'[5] Marx believed that his doctrine would stand or fall according to its empirical effectiveness. One cannot prove his innocence by simply finding in his texts value judgements which contradict the value systems established in 'actually existing' communist societies. As Kolakowski points out:

> It is easy to see that Marx had never written anything to the effect that the socialist kingdom of freedom would consist in one-party despotic rule; that he did not reject democratic forms of social life; that he expected from socialism the abolition of economical coercion.

If this is true, Kolakowski continues, it still may be true 'that there are logical reasons why his theory implies consequences incompatible with his ostensible value judgments'; for 'some previously unnoticed or neglected empirical connections' may make 'the implementation of one part of the utopia possible only at the price of denying other ingredients'.[6] This is just a common-sense triviality, but it is amazing how many defenders of Marx ignore it in their efforts to keep his ideas in a state of perpetual purity, unsullied by the mud of history.

Other, more convincing Marxist apologists, accepting the link between theory and practice, admit the relevance of empirical evidence and try to explain *why* the various communist experiments have gone wrong. Influenced by Trotsky's account of Stalinism, they remind us that revolutions inspired by Marx have occurred only in countries that were economically backward and therefore unprepared for a genuine proletarian revolution of the kind envisaged by Marx, a revolution carried out by literate industrial workers, who would constitute the 'immense majority' of society, a revolution designed to spread *existing* wealth, not to modernize a primitive productive base. Thus, in the opinion of John Kautsky

---

[5] *Writings of the Young Marx on Philosophy and Society*, trans. and ed. L. D. Easton and K. H. Guddat (New York: Doubleday, 1967), 401.

[6] L. Kolakowski, 'Marxist Roots of Stalinism', in *Stalinism*, ed. R. C. Tucker (New York: W. W. Norton, 1977), 283–4.

(grandson of the great Karl), not just Stalinism but Leninism 'was a perversion or misunderstanding of Marxism ... an adaptation of an ideology born in an industrial environment to the conditions of an underdeveloped one'.[7] For such observers, Marxism, notwithstanding its practical deformations, 'still remains the expression of epochal critical consciousness'.[8]

It would of course be foolish to disregard the impact of events and circumstances on Marxist revolutions. No society has ever been entirely begotten by an ideology; no society is simply produced by ideas conceived before its existence; no society can escape the influence of its past history. Yet the circumstantial explanation of communist repression does not withstand scrutiny. Contrary to the implicit assumption made by Marx's defenders, there is no necessary correlation between political despotism and lack of economic development. Russia in 1917 was no less developed than Italy, and the latter possessed a functioning—albeit corrupt—liberal parliamentary system, one stretching back to the Risorgimento. Modern-day Costa Rica is, on most measures, an underdeveloped country; and yet it shines out like a beacon of tolerance and liberal democracy. And what about India, self-proclaimed standard-bearer of the Third World, which, since independence in the late 1940s, has seldom deviated from the principles and procedures of parliamentary government? Conversely, two of the most repressive of former communist states, East Germany and Czechoslovakia, could hardly be described as under-developed at any time during their long and sad association with Marxism-Leninism. Neither can the economic backward-ness argument account for the sheer *scale* of communist tyranny. Triumphant Marxist revolutionaries have not simply failed to realize their democratic goals; they have somehow contrived to bring about the absolute negation of those goals. Of the four most murderous despots in modern history, no less than three—Stalin, Mao, and Pol Pot—were self-professed Marxists.

It is hard to escape the conclusion that Marxism itself, by virtue of its method or its message, and despite its proclama-

---

[7] *Communism and the Politics of Development, Persistent Myths and Changing Behaviour* (New York: Wiley, 1968), 42.

[8] M. Marković, 'Stalinism and Marxism', in *Stalinism*, 318.

tions of democratic faith, is largely responsible for the repression carried out in its name. But let me be clear: it is not my intention to deny the obvious fact that communism as we know it is/was, to some degree, a product of its historical context, a 'mutation'[9] of classical Marxism. In evaluating the origins of communist authoritarianism, we must, in Kolakowski's helpful analogy, separate the 'genetic' from the 'environmental' factors:

To say that the 'genes' (inherited ideology) were entirely responsible for the actual shape of the child would obviously be as silly as to state that this shape is to be exclusively accounted for by 'environment', i.e., contingent historical events.[10]

There have broadly been three ways of explaining the 'genetic' link between Marxism and authoritarianism. Each claims to find a fatal flaw in the doctrine: either its economic dogma, or its consequentialism, or its supposed messianism. In what follows I shall outline these arguments and point to some weaknesses that make them less than wholly adequate. I shall then set out and justify my own explanation, which holds that Marxism's Achilles' heel, the underlying cause of its deformity in practice, is its holistic conception of man.

The first type of explanation focuses on the consequences of central planning, itself necessitated by the abolition of both private property and the market mechanism. While normally associated with defenders of capitalism, anxious warnings about the authoritarian potential of state socialism were first delivered by leading anarchist thinkers, long before the Russian Revolution. Writing in 1872, Michael Bakunin had a prophetic vision of the proletarian dictatorship:

There will therefore be no longer any privileged class, but there will be a government, and, note this well, an extremely complex government, which will not content itself with governing and administering the masses politically, as all governments do today, but which will also administer them economically, concentrating in its own hands the production and the just division of wealth, the cultivation of land, the establishment and development of factories, the organisation and direction of commerce, finally the application of capital to pro-

---

[9] D. Shub, *Lenin* (Harmondsworth, Middx.: Penguin, 1966), 10.
[10] 'Marxist Roots of Stalinism', in *Stalinism*, 297.

duction by the only banker, the State. All that will demand an immense knowledge and many 'heads overflowing with brains' in this government. It will be the reign of *scientific intelligence*, the most aristocratic, despotic, arrogant and contemptuous of all regimes. There will be a new class, a new hierarchy of real and pretended scientists and scholars, and the world will be divided into a minority ruling in the name of knowledge and an immense ignorant majority. And then, woe betide the mass of ignorant ones![11]

Substantially the same argument has been developed by conservatives and classical liberals, whose most distinguished spokesman in this century has perhaps been F. A. Hayek. In his famous work, *The Road to Serfdom*, first published in 1944, he baldly states that 'a directed economy must be run on more or less dictatorial lines'. He then elaborates:

That the complex system of interrelated activities, if it is to be consciously directed at all, must be directed by a single staff of experts, and that ultimate responsibility and power must rest in the hands of a commander-in-chief, whose actions must not be fettered by democratic procedure, is too obvious a consequence of underlying ideas of central planning not to command fairly general assent.[12]

Hayek offers no serious arguments to support this 'obvious' assertion, which may not seem obvious to everyone. We can of course concede, as a matter of fact, that all planned economies have been run on dictatorial lines, but this empirical correlation in itself tells us nothing about a causal link. In particular, it is important to recognize that all comprehensively planned economies in this century have been Marxist in inspiration, so the reason for dictatorship may lie in some feature of Marxism other than central planning. This is a question of simple logic. What Hayek does is to explain why central planning of the kind that eliminates economic competition is bound to curtail individual choice in the service of such abstractions as the 'common good' or the 'public interest'. What he does not do (or even attempt) is to show us why the imposition of collective goals or values requires 'a commander-in-chief whose actions must not be fettered

---

[11] *Marxism, Freedom and the State*, trans. and ed. K. J. Kenafick (London: Freedom Press, 1984), 38.

[12] *The Road to Serfdom* (London: Routledge and Kegan Paul, 1976), 66.

by democratic procedure'. Let us take a closer look at his position.

The crux of the argument is that economic planning necessitates deliberate discrimination between the particular wants and needs of different groups and persons:

When we have to choose between higher wages for nurses or doctors and more extensive services for the sick, more milk for children and better wages for agricultural workers, or between employment for the unemployed or better wages for those already employed, nothing short of a complete system of values in which every want of every person or group has a definite place is necessary to provide an answer.[13]

Individuals would not be allowed to live in accordance with *their own* 'system of values'; the planning authority 'would use its power to assist some ends and prevent the realisation of others'.[14] Hayek insists that economic control 'is not merely control of a sector of human life which can be separated from the rest; it is the control of the means for all our ends'. The planners must 'determine which ends are to be served, which values are to be rated higher and which lower, in short, what men should believe and strive for'. Economic planning would therefore 'involve direction of almost the whole of our life'.[15] This seems an absurd exaggeration. Economic planners would not necessarily tell individual citizens which God to worship, or even which occupation to pursue. Still, planning must, by definition, entail the imposition of collective priorities in areas that could be left to the free play of market forces. To those who point to the 'wage slavery' of the free enterprise system, or to the arbitrary and mysterious workings of the market mechanism, Hayek offers two arguments. First, our 'freedom of choice in a competitive society rests on the fact that, if one person refuses to satisfy our wishes we can turn to another', whereas 'if we face a monopolist we are at his mercy'. And an authority directing the *whole* economic system would be 'the most powerful monopolist conceivable'.[16]

---

[13] Ibid. 58.
[14] Ibid. 70.
[15] Ibid. 68–9.
[16] Ibid. 69.

Secondly, Hayek underlines the sheer complexity of central authoritative planning, which makes it impossible to take account of individual likes and dislikes. The planning authority must take all possible measures to simplify its mind-boggling task, thus further diminishing individual choice:

> To make this immense task manageable it will have to reduce the diversity of human capacities and inclinations to a few categories of readily interchangeable units and deliberately to disregard minor personal differences.[17]

Hayek associates individual choice with individual rights: the restriction of one means the restriction of the other. State socialism, he maintains, must ride roughshod over the most basic human rights, for these would inevitably obstruct the planning process. How could freedom of property (including property in one's labour) be secured in a system of total planning? How could freedom of the press be safeguarded when the supply of paper and all the channels of distribution are controlled by the planning authority?[18] Here Hayek, in peremptory fashion, blurs a crucial distinction between different kinds of rights. Socialist planning does, of necessity, rule out private property in the means of production on any but the smallest scale. The freedom to enter into contracts would also be severely curtailed, as would (one supposes) the mobility of labour. From a liberal perspective, then, socialist planning would certainly abridge the rights of man. But is the right to property really essential to democratic accountability? Can we not have free elections and referenda in the absence of such a right? It may be that the institution of private property, by ensuring a plurality of power centres, presents a formidable barrier to the abuse of political power. Against this apparently commonsensical view, we must balance the fact that this century abounds with military and fascist dictatorships, almost all of them based on capitalist or quasi-feudal modes of production. Alas, great property owners are not averse to supporting despotic regimes when democracy poses a threat to their vested interests. *Both* capitalism and state socialism are susceptible to despotic political administration. In addi-

---

[17] Ibid. 72.
[18] Ibid. 63–4.

tion, Tocqueville made the valid point, a century and a half ago, that democracy in its purest form rests on one source of power, the people, which 'has the right to do whatever it pleases'. As democracy progresses, 'the idea of intermediate powers is weakened' and 'the idea of the omnipotence and sole authority of society at large rises to fill its place'.[19] Whether or not this is desirable or conducive to individual freedom, the fact remains that democracy can exist where there are no countervailing powers. But it is not, in any case, clear why a socialist society should be unable to accommodate a diversity of independent power centres: local government, trade unions, churches, industrial and professional associations. All these organizations and institutions could, through entrenched constitutional principles and rights, have their say in the planning process and use their influence to check state power. Free enterprise is far from being the only 'intermediate power', and it is hard to see why it should be deemed a necessary condition, rather than simply a facilitating factor, of democratic pluralism. As Joseph Schumpeter, no lover of socialism, has observed, 'democracy has nothing to do with ... the "freedoms" with which the economist is concerned, the freedom of investment, the freedom of consumer choice, and the freedom of occupational choice'.[20]

Freedom of the press, however, *would* seem to be required if democracy is to exist in anything but name. Where certain viewpoints are suppressed, democratic debate cannot be said to flourish; and without such debate elections or plebiscites are meaningless, except as propaganda exercises. But is it necessarily true that state control over the supply of paper and network of distribution negates freedom of the press? The most Hayek can say is that state socialism provides resources for suppression. In Britain the BBC is, for all intents and purposes, owned and regulated by the state. But in its news and current affairs programmes it assiduously presents all shades of opinion. This is more than can be said for the privately owned print media, which are almost uniformly

[19] A. de Tocqueville, *Democracy in America*, ii, ed. P. Bradley (New York: Vintage Books, 1945), 307–8.
[20] *Capitalism, Socialism and Democracy*, 3rd edn. (New York: Harper & Row, 1950), 229, 411.

hostile to the Labour Party. Indeed, in right-wing dictator-ships, privately owned newspapers are as servile as their state-owned counterparts in communist countries. Of course, if the planning process is controlled by an unaccountable and un-representative clique, then they most assuredly will use their power to stifle free expression. But there is no reason in principle why a democratic electorate should impose such restrictions on debate. Hayek's argument that comprehensive planning will destroy a free press assumes precisely what it should be trying to prove: that the logic of state planning rules out democratic accountability. If it is argued, by way of rejoinder, that I am too sanguine about the tolerance of the mass public, I need only point out that an intolerant democ-ratic citizenry can perfectly well enforce its censorship in the absence of socialism. The McCarthyite period in America was proof of this. Experience teaches us that repressive laws, sack-ing of dissidents, blacklisting, etc. are all perfectly compatible with a free-market economy. Unencumbered public debate is guaranteed by a democratic political *culture*, by widespread diffusion of democratic habits and values; while such a cul-ture may be encouraged by certain economic arrangements, only a crude determinist would argue that it is *tied* to those arrangements. Relish the irony: a major criticism of Marxism's democratic credentials would seem to depend upon one of Marxism's least tenable theses: namely, that mass psychology is crucially shaped by the economic structure.

In the end Hayek must fall back on the contention that the massive complexity of central economic planning requires an all-powerful bureaucracy, staffed by experts ('heads overflow-ing with brains', as Bakunin described them) and distinguished by a hierarchical command structure. Here we are reminded of Weber's prediction that Marxism would lead to 'the dicta-torship of the official and not that of the worker'.[21] This analysis has a certain plausibility. Under conditions of total planning, bureaucratic experts will unavoidably play an active role in policy formation. But—and again we take note of Hayek's tendency to blur distinctions—need this be an *all-*

---

[21] *From Max Weber: Essays in Sociology*, ed. H. H. Gerth and C. Wright Mills (London: Routledge and Kegan Paul, 1970), cited on p. 50 of the Intro-duction by the editors.

powerful role, immune to democratic control? Surely it would be possible for the planning authority to specify a range of feasible, internally consistent plans, which could then be submitted to a democratic decision-making procedure—though the execution of the resultant decisions would necessarily leave plenty of scope for administrative discretion at the level of detail. To say this is not to indulge in the participatory fantasies of the council communists and their descendants, who saw (or see) no contradiction between comprehensive central planning and worker or communal self-management. It is not, however, beyond the wit of man to devise a practicable system in which major planning decisions are responsive to the wishes of the people's elected representatives. There is no reason why different candidates or political parties could not attach themselves to different plans, embodying different priorities. Once the collective choice is made, individual choice will probably be more limited than in a market system, for the reasons given by Hayek. But democracy is about the sovereignty of the people (or the majority), not the sovereignty of the individual. It is paradoxical to argue that democracy turns into its opposite once it extends beyond the narrowly political dimension of human endeavour. While comprehensive planning may not be compatible with *liberal* democracy, based as it is on private property and contractual relations, such planning is, in principle at least, compatible with democracy of a more traditional and far-reaching kind, where popular control penetrates the economic sphere.

A more convincing approach to understanding Marxist dictatorship is to examine the presuppositions of what Steven Lukes calls Marxism's 'morality of emancipation'. To illustrate the nature of this morality he draws a distinction between deontological and consequentialist theories.[22] According to the former, 'right' behaviour is determined by reference to transhistorical principles, such as justice, or natural law, or human rights, or the will of God. Consequentialism, in contrast, judges actions by their empirical consequences only—morality descends from heaven to earth and becomes a subject of scientific analysis. Different types of consequentialism will

---

[22] *Marxism and Morality* (Oxford: Clarendon Press, 1985), 142.

value different types of consequences. For the classical utilitarians the standard was the 'greatest happiness of the greatest number', the maximization of pleasure. If we take Marxism to be a form of consequentialism, the criterion of evaluation is 'history'. An action is right to the extent that it promotes the realization of the imminent and immanent goal of world history: communism, 'the riddle of history solved', a realm of perfection where individual self-actualization is combined with flawless social harmony.

In seeking to explain the brutality and authoritarianism of supposedly Marxist regimes, some critics would look no further than the consequentialist character of Marxist thinking, with its implicit (and sometimes explicit) premiss that 'the end justifies the means'. As Rubashov, the fictional hero of *Darkness at Noon*, reflects at the end of the novel: 'We have thrown overboard all conventions, our sole guiding principle is that of consequent logica; we are sailing without ethical ballast. Perhaps the heart of the evil lay there.'[23] Merleau-Ponty, in his discourse on the Moscow trials, explains how Marxist consequentialism can lead to the silencing or punishment of people who are, in Western eyes, innocent of any crime:

> political acts are to be judged not only according to their meaning for the moral agent but also according to the sense they acquire in the historical context and dialectical phase in which such acts originate. Moreover, it is impossible to see how a Communist could disavow this approach, as it is essential to Marxist thought. In a world of struggle—and for Marxists history is the history of class struggles—there is no margin of indifferent action which classical thought accords to individuals; for every action unfolds and we are responsible for its consequences.... [I]n a period of revolutionary tension or external threat there is no clear-cut boundary between political divergences and objective treason.[24]

When a revolutionary regime equates 'political divergence' with 'objective treason', it might just as well pronounce a

---

[23] A Koestler, *Darkness at Noon* (Harmondsworth, Middx.: Penguin, 1964), 206.
[24] M. Merleau-Ponty, *Humanism and Terror*, trans. J. O'Neill (Boston: Beacon Press, 1969), 33–4.

formal anathema over free debate. Plekhanov, in a memorable speech, expanded on this theme:

Every democratic principle must be considered not by itself, abstractly, but in relation to what may be called the fundamental principle of democracy, namely *salus populi suprema lex*. Translated into the language of the revolutionist, this means that the success of the revolution is the highest law. And if the success of the revolution demanded a temporary limitation of the working of this or that democratic principle, then it would be criminal to refrain from such a limitation.[25]

For the consequentialist, democratic practices are of contingent value only; they, like all other forms of action, must be judged in terms of the ultimate goal. It is difficult, though, to see how consequentialism as such can account for Marxist dictatorship. The classical utilitarians are universally acclaimed as founders of liberal democracy, and they were unremitting defenders of majority rule and free expression. It would seem that the real threat to freedom and democracy lies not so much in Marxist consequentialism as in the nature of the Marxist goal itself.

With this consideration in mind, some commentators have discovered the roots of Marxist authoritarianism in its 'political messianism', which, according to J. L. Talmon's classic definition, 'postulates a preordained, harmonious and perfect scheme of things, to which men are irresistibly driven', and which finds freedom 'in the pursuit and attainment of an absolute collective purpose'.[26] Marxism began with scientific pretensions, but—in the opinion of critics like Talmon—it soon degenerated into a vulgar and secular religion, weighed

---

[25] G. V. Plekhanov, Speech to the Second Congress of the RSDLP (1903), trans. T. Cliff, in *Lenin*, vol. i, *Building the Party* (London: Pluto Press, 1975), 106. Listen to Gramsci's chilling variant of Plekhanov's principle: 'The modern Prince [the communist party] . . . revolutionises the whole system of intellectual and moral relations, in that its development means precisely that any given act is seen as useful or harmful, as virtuous or as wicked, only in so far as it has as its point of reference the modern Prince itself, and helps to strengthen or oppose it. In men's consciences, the Prince takes the place of the Divinity or the categorical imperative.' (*Selections from the Prison Notebooks*, ed. and trans. Q. Hoare and G. Nowell Smith (London: Lawrence and Wishart, 1971), 133).

[26] J. L. Talmon, *The Origins of Totalitarian Democracy* (Harmondsworth, Middx.: Penguin, 1987), 2 (first pub. 1952).

down by a dubious eschatology. An early proponent of this thesis was Benedetto Croce, who defined Marxism as 'substantially a theological and medieval vision, strongly coloured by Judaic apocalyptic thinking'.[27] Like all religions, it has its sacred texts and transcendent metaphysics on the one hand, and its myths and popular simplifications on the other. The parallels with Christianity at least are obvious enough: Marx = Jesus; the proletariat = God; the capitalist class = the devil; communism = heaven; capitalism = hell. And so forth. As with all religions, empirical thinking and free criticism are replaced by faith, by a priori reasoning, which must be accepted whatever the evidence of the senses. Those who question the scriptures, or their authoritative interpretation, are labelled heretics, liable to ostracism or worse. And, in common with all religions, Marxism appeals to an instinct deeply embedded in human nature: the yearning for salvation, for immersion in the stream of universal life.

But what, in this view, makes Marxism more dangerous than conventional religion is its assumption that heaven can be realized on earth, in an apocalyptic denouement of the historical drama. To Talmon, this 'longing for a final resolution of all contradictions and conflicts into a state of total harmony' is incompatible with 'both the diversity which goes with a multiplicity of social groups, and the diversity resulting from human spontaneity and empiricism'. What is more, the messianic vision 'runs counter to the lessons of nature and history', for these 'show civilization as the evolution of a multiplicity of historically and pragmatically formed clusters of social existence and social endeavour, and not as the achievement of abstract Man on a single level of existence'.[28] Invariably, the great mass of people, with their particularistic loyalties and indifference to abstractions, wish only to be left in peace to pursue their own diverse occupations. This apathy exasperates their self-appointed saviours, who conclude—with absurd metaphysical hubris—that the inarticulate masses have been lulled and deceived by their oppressors. As sure as night follows day, we then get the arrogant distinction between the

[27] *Cultura e vita morale* (Bari: Laterza, 1955), 286.
[28] *The Origins of Totalitarian Democracy*, 250, 254.

people's spontaneously expressed wishes and their *real*, or authentic, wishes, which, needless to say, correspond to what is 'good' for them. The discovery of these secret wishes, lurking just beneath the surface, gives the vanguard, the inspired prophets, 'a blank cheque to act on behalf of the people, without reference to the people's actual will'.[29] The essential thing is not to let the people be free to act as they like, but to do the right thing, as understood by those who claim the virtue of knowing what is exclusively right and good for the people. For Talmon, Marxism is simply the latest variant of political messianism, which he traces back to the Jacobins of the French Revolution. Quoting Babeuf's apologia for Robespierre's dictatorship, he illustrates how the quest for earthly salvation leads to self-righteous fanaticism:

The salvation of 25,000,000 men cannot be weighed against consideration for a few shady individuals. A regenerator must take broad views. He must mow down all that impedes him, all that cumbers his path, all that might hinder his safe arrival at the goal he has set before him.[30]

For this goal represents the full realization of freedom: the Promethean construction of a Perfect City.

This interpretation of Marxism as a form of pernicious messianism suffers from a crucial weakness: it is almost impossible to find a Marxist who would recognize himself in the portrait drawn by Talmon and those like him. Marxists have always seen themselves as social scientists, building generalizations and discovering 'laws' on the basis of empirical observation. While a person's self-image may be false, there *is* undoubtedly a strand of 'realistic Marxism', stretching from Kautsky to the Eurocommunists, which singularly fails to display millennial aspirations. One could, I suppose, argue that all or almost all Marxists are at least implicitly messianic—fundamentalist theologians despite their scientific or pragmatic rhetoric. Even this, however, seems inadequate as a description of, say, Brezhnev and his dark-suited clones throughout Eastern Europe. They certainly exhibited a deep-seated desire for social regimentation and conformity; but did

---

[29] Ibid. 48.
[30] Ibid. 220.

they really believe in the possibility of an earthly paradise? Did they really harbour an ill-proportioned passion for the abstract? Perhaps, as the Trotskyists never tire of telling us, these faceless party bosses were not true Marxists. But this exclusion raises the most appalling terminological difficulties, and, in any case, it is precisely the repression carried out by these men that we are trying to explain. If we accept that they were not Marxists, then we are obliged to concede that Marxism itself may not be the problem. While messianism must form part of any explanation of Marxist authoritarianism I think there is another, less contentious feature of Marxism that underlies the thoughts and deeds of all professed Marxists whatever their orientation: messianic, scientific, or simply bureaucratic. I am referring—as mentioned earlier—to Marxism's holistic conception of man. Allow me to elaborate.

Although he occasionally lapsed into 'old-speak' terminology to convey his vision of human excellence ('man is a species-being', etc.),[31] Marx categorically rejected all theories that began from the 'intrinsic nature' of individuals, whether this nature was conceived in transcendental (e.g. Christian) or naturalistic (e.g. Hobbesian) terms. For him, human nature (in the descriptive sense) was inseparable from its specific cultural setting. According to the sixth Thesis on Feuerbach, 'the essence of man is no abstraction inhering in each single individual. In its actuality, it is the ensemble of social relationships.'[32] Elsewhere, Marx writes: '... *man* is not an abstract being squatting outside the world. Man is the *world of men*, the state, society.'[33] From these passages we can gather that Marx's critique of essentialism was also a critique of the bourgeois tendency to fix on the individual as the theoretically primary element of social analysis. Marx fundamentally opposed the abstract individualism of classical liberal theory, which viewed society as an aggregate of self-directing individuals, atomistically detached from their social context. As he maintained in the *Grundrisse*: 'Society does not consist of individuals, but expresses the sum of inter-relations, the rela-

---

[31] See Chapter 2, pp. 22–4.

[32] *Writings of the Young Marx*, 402.

[33] 'Towards the Critique of Hegel's Philosophy of Law: Introduction', in *Writings of the Young Marx*, 250.

tions within which these individuals stand.'[34] Individuals, in other words, are not the creators of their relations but rather 'the bearers' or 'the embodiments' of those relations.[35] Whereas the bourgeois philosophers, notably Hobbes and Locke, posited a disjunction between the social whole and the human personality, Marx saw the collectivity as constitutive of the human agent's core identity; the individual is merely a locus of intersecting social relationships, which give him meaning and significance. 'To be avoided above all', Marx tells us, 'is establishing "society" once again as an abstraction over against the individual.' Contrary to the theoretical fictions of liberalism, there is no hiatus between the individual's self-consciousness and the external system of social phenomena: 'The individual *is* the *social being. . . .* The individual and generic life of man are not *distinct*'.[36] To regard men and women as isolated market units is to see the human race in mystified form, to fail to see it for what it really is, the product of social interdependence. And the individual, be it noted, is a product of society in the literal sense, for Marx is saying that human identity can be reduced, without remainder, to 'the ensemble of social relationships'. In his view, all talk of a 'unique self', a primitive datum beyond social definition, was 'imaginary' and 'abstract', a derivative of Christian nonsense about immaterial 'souls'.[37] For man is the 'totality', whose '*human* relations to the world—seeing, hearing, smelling, tasting, feeling, thinking, perceiving, sensing, wishing, acting, loving . . . are immediately communal in form'.[38]

[34] K. Marx, *Grundrisse*, trans. M. Nicolaus (Harmondsworth, Middx.: Penguin, 1973), 265.

[35] Preface to the first edition of *Capital*, in *Marx & Engels: Basic Writings on Politics and Philosophy*, ed. L. S. Feuer (New York: Doubleday, 1959), 136–7. See also *The German Ideology*, in *Writings of the Young Marx*, where Marx insists that individual personality 'depends on' (p. 409) or is 'determined by' (p. 458) material conditions.

[36] *Economic and Philosophic Manuscripts* (1844), in *Writings of the Young Marx*, 306.

[37] *The German Ideology*, in *The Collected Works of Marx and Engels*, v (London: Lawrence and Wishart, from 1975), 120.

[38] *Economic and Philosophic Manuscripts* (1844), in *Writings of the Young Marx*, 307. In his third Thesis on Feuerbach, however, Marx *seems* to retreat from social determinism. The relevant passage reads as follows: 'The materialistic doctrine concerning the change of circumstances and education forgets that circumstances are changed by men and that the educator must

The best way to discuss the implications of Marx's holistic concept of humanity is to break it down into three different aspects: the ontological, the epistemological, and the ethical. Let us look at each one in turn.

First, the ontological aspect. Marx, by viewing human beings as nothing other than the expression of social forces, refused to acknowledge the distinct identity of the individual as an agent whose experiences or interests or personal projects resist incorporation under global headings. The Marxist trait of identifying people in terms of roles and categories is firmly based in Marx's disinclination to see individuals as unique selves with their own separate and independent points of view. Now, if the individual is social in the innermost depths of his being, how can we plausibly sustain the conviction that he is an end-in-himself, a creature of irreducible value, whose opinions and aspirations must be respected simply because

himself be educated. Hence this doctrine must divide society into two parts —one of which towers above.' (p. 401). Marx was here alluding to the view, common to both French materialists and Utopian socialists, that people are formed by circumstances. It follows that a change in people requires a change in these circumstances. But the classical environmentalists came up against the inconvenient fact that circumstances are themselves necessarily changed by people. The stock way out of this closed circle was to assume (at least in effect) that some people are exempt from the total conditioning by circumstances, and these are the ones whose mission it is to change the latter in such a way as to change the mass of people. In this sense, society is divided into 'two parts'—one 'superior' and the other, by implication, inferior. As Wal Suchting convincingly argues, Marx intended to attack the *inconsistency* of the bourgeois materialists and the early socialists, not social determinism as such. According to him, these thinkers, the traditional materialists in particular, made the mistake of sharply separating individuals from their social relations, which were conceived as being purely external to them. As we learn in the sixth Thesis, Feuerbach, a representative of this erroneous mode of thought, presupposed 'an abstract—*isolated*—human individual' (p. 402). Contrariwise, Marx attributes primacy to 'the ensemble of social relations' which confers on individuals definite characteristics, motives for action, and the rest. Furthermore (to quote Suchting), 'these relational structures have inbuilt tendencies to change—basically, "contradictions"—which express themselves, work themselves out, through the people who stand in the relations, and in particular through their actions'. Thus, on the one hand, circumstances (social relations) *are* shaped by people; but, on the other hand, people's ideas are determined by the changing relations. Marx thus escaped from the vicious circle by abandoning every vestige of abstract individualism. See W. Suchting, 'Marx's Theses on Feuerbach', in *Issues in Marxist Philosophy*, ii, ed. J. Mepham and D. H. Ruben (Brighton: Harvester, 1979), 12–16, 19–20.

they are his own? How can we reconcile Marx's insistence on the social nature of personal identity with the idea of an individual who creates his or her own identity by acts of personal choice? Personal autonomy would seem to require what Marxism, as a philosophy, cannot accommodate: a 'private space' within which human beings can stand back from prevailing images, usages, and values. Marx's attack on the rights of man is instructive in this respect. Like the classical utilitarians, he dismissed them as empty abstractions, 'nonsense upon stilts', in Jeremy Bentham's pithy formulation.[39] But, unlike the utilitarians, Marx also condemned them as *individualistic* abstractions, as 'only the rights ... of egoistic man, man separated from other men and from the community ... man withdrawn into himself, his private interest and his private choice'. On this account, the doctrine of human rights presupposes an atomistic conception of the world, which pictures man 'as an isolated monad', abstractly counterposed to society.[40] Marx understood that inherent in the idea of a right is the assumption that individual claims must take priority over collective needs. Or, to put it another way, socialist construction must be subordinated to individual freedom. He was clear that this type of individualism rested upon erroneous metaphysical foundations. This explains his contempt for the liberal belief that liberty is 'the right to do and perform anything that does not harm others'. In his estimation, liberty so defined is 'the right of the *limited* individual limited to himself'.[41] It is the right of selfishness.

Of course, Marx and later Marxists wanted an individuality of sorts. They repeatedly insisted that man is most at home with himself when he is developing and exercising his particular creative talents. Communism would encourage 'universally developed individuals'[42]; the 'new socialist man' would be an active agent, 'cultivating his gifts in all directions'.[43] As Kolakowski rightly indicates, the Marxist vision

---

[39] 'Anarchical Fallacies', in *Nonsense upon Stilts: Bentham, Burke and Marx on the Rights of Man*, ed. J. Waldron (London: Methuen, 1987), 53.

[40] 'On the Jewish Question', in *Writings of the Young Marx*, 235, 237.

[41] Ibid. 235.

[42] K. Marx, *Grundrisse*, 162.

[43] K. Marx, *The German Ideology*, in *Collected Works of Marx and Engels*, v, 77–8.

was modelled 'on pictures of universal giants of the Hellenic and Renaissance worlds rather than on the patterns of barracks and monasteries'.[44] Yet, as we have seen, Marxists also assert that the human individual is a passive imprint of social forms, a creature whose cognitive and motivational personality is shaped by his/her social position. Where, then, is the space for autonomous choice? How can we posit the existence of *distinctive* psychological qualities—those that express our individuality by setting us apart from others in a similar social position? While 'universally developed individuals' may be the explicit goal of communism, Marxian metaphysics, as G. W. Smith points out, renders nonsensical 'the idea of an individual who creates his own identity by acts of social choice'.[45] The apparent contradiction may be resolved if we consider the nature of Marxist individuality. It has nothing to do with defining one's own identity. Nor is it a matter of personal independence, which Marxists consistently denigrate. Gramsci, for example, dismissed individualism (in this sense) as 'a brutish element', and contrasted it unfavourably with community spirit, which he alarmingly identified with 'party spirit'.[46] For Marx, as for Hegel before him, true freedom emerges from a dialectical self-identity between subject and object, whereby the conditions governing the self both express and constitute the self. In Hegel's metaphysics, however, the self was universalized or abstractly conceived as an all-embracing *Geist*, detached from empirically individuated persons. In bringing Hegel 'down to earth' Marx applied the dialectic to the individual physical subjects and concrete social conditions of a communist society. As such conditions would not be external to the individual, they could not be said to impede his or her free creativity. Marx and his followers therefore saw no incompatibility between individual

[44] L. Kolakowski, 'The Myth of Human Self-Identity', in *The Socialist Idea*, ed. L. Kolakowski and S. Hampshire (London: Weidenfeld and Nicolson, 1974), 24.

[45] 'Marxian Metaphysics and Individual Freedom', in *Marx and Marxisms*, ed. G. H. R. Parkinson (Cambridge: Cambridge University Press, 1982), 241. Smith claims (p. 242) that Marx's fragmentation of the individual self of 'common sense' amounted to a 'conceptual revolution'.

[46] *Selections from the Prison Notebooks*, 147. See also K. Marx, *Grundrisse*, 80–2.

self-expression and submission to collectively determined purposes or practices. The Marxist paradigm of individuality is
not that of the lone dissenter, standing out from the crowd
and challenging social verities; rather, it is a sculptor at work,
using his socially nurtured talents to fashion objects for the
enjoyment of his fellow human beings. The development and
expression of his/her creative abilities must be subordinated
to the collective good and subjected to communal control.
For, apart from being creative, 'man' is, after all, a 'social
animal', a 'species-being'. '[W]hat I make from myself', Marx
once wrote, 'I make for society, conscious of my nature as
social.'[47] Marxists sacrifice the autonomous dimensions of
personhood to the communal aspects of species-being.[48] Individuality of the kind desired by Marx and his disciples has
no need of liberty as defined by the French Declaration of
1791: 'the power to do anything which does not harm others'.
Nor does it need any other human right for that matter. For
individuality and conformity are seen as two sides of the
same coin. As della Volpe put it, true freedom involves 'social
recognition' of 'personal qualities and capacities'.[49] Essential
to Marxist individuality is not a person's judgement of the
world but the world's judgement of him.[50]

[47] Economic and Philosophic Manuscripts (1844), in Writings of the Young
Marx, 306.
[48] But, in a curious book, D. F. B. Tucker asserts that Marx refused 'to
accept that the purposes and values of actual individuals be subordinated to
the claims of the collectivity'. Instead, he wanted persons to be 'left free to
realize aims which they have decided upon for themselves'. He thought it
illegitimate to promote his 'own distinctive conception of the good' at the
cost of violating individual freedom. Marx was therefore unquestionably an
'individualist', who placed 'great value on the achievement of autonomy'.
Tucker presents not a single piece of textual evidence to verify this surprising
interpretation. It seems to have been arrived at through pseudo-logical derivation from an undeniable truth: Marx's desire for the fullest development of
individual potentialities. Of course, Marx wanted individuals to be 'left free
to realize aims which they have decided upon for themselves' only if these
aims coincided with the collectively defined needs of a communist society.
To describe this as 'individualism' rather than 'collectivism' would seem to
be a perverse misuse of language; and one, it must be said, that cannot be
blamed on Marx himself, who never tried to conceal his collectivist priorities
(Marxism and Individualism (Oxford: Basil Blackwell, 1980), 59, 65).
[49] G. della Volpe, 'Comunismo e democrazia moderna', in Rousseau e
Marx (Rome: Riuniti, 1957), 53.
[50] The difficulty of squaring Marxist 'individualism' with individualism as
it has normally been understood in the history of political thought is well

From the standpoint of the individual, the Benthamite rejection of human rights is much less ominous than that of the Marxists, for the utilitarian stress on the pluralism of individual natures, on the special qualities that differentiate one person from another, operates as a functional equivalent to rights. In common with all liberals, the utilitarians were committed to what Richard Vernon has called 'the notion of distinctness', to the 'understanding that each person acts for reasons that are compelling to him or her and which are not subsumable under some role which someone else may wish to assign'.[51] A respect for individual choice flows logically from this understanding. To quote J. S. Mill: 'If a person possesses any tolerable amount of common sense and experience, his own mode of laying out his existence is the best, not because it is the best in itself, but because it is his own mode.'[52] Once we depart from the assumption of distinct and autonomous individuals, and instead assume, as do Marxists, that (post-revolutionary) society is a single organic unit, informed by a common spirit, then it makes sense to leave decisions about how we should live to those with superior skills and insight. Neither individual choice nor, indeed, individual existence can any longer be accorded supreme value. Merleau-Ponty touches upon the connection between ontology and political values in his analysis of Marxist violence and repression:

where each conscience is a totality unto itself, the violence done to a single conscience would suffice . . . to damn the society that caused

exemplified in the contorted prose of Karol Kosik, who tries to explain why Marxist man 'remains an individual even in the collective': 'Individuality is neither an addition nor an unexplainable irrational remainder to which the individual is reduced after subtracting the social relations, historical contexts and so on. If the individual is deprived of his social mask and underneath there is no hint of an individual appearance, this privation bears witness only to the worthlessness of his individuality, not to his nonexistence' ('The Individual and History', in *Marx and the Western World*, ed. N. Lobkowicz (Notre Dame: University of Notre Dame Press, 1967), 189). What this apparently contradictory statement means is anyone's guess. Mind-numbing obscurity, we can safely say, is the last refuge of a scholar with a weak case.

[51] 'Moral Pluralism and the Liberal Mind', in *Unity, Plurality and Politics: Essays in Honour of F. M. Barnard*, ed. J. M. Porter and R. Vernon (London: Croom Helm, 1986), 157.

[52] 'On Liberty', in *Utilitarianism, Liberty, and Representative Government* (London: Dent, 1910), 125.

it. There would be no sense in preferring a regime which employed violence for humanist aims since from the viewpoint of the conscience which suffers it, violence is absolutely unacceptable, being the negation of conscience; and in such a philosophy there can be no other standpoint than that of self-consciousness, the world and history being only the sum of such viewpoints. But these are precisely the axioms that Marxism, following Hegel, questions by introducing the perspective of one consciousness upon another. What we find in the private life of a couple, or in a society of friends, or, with all the more reason, in history, is not a series of juxtaposed 'self-consciousnesses'.[53]

For utilitarians, in contrast, human collectivities are reducible to their individual components, or—in Merleau-Ponty's terms —their individual 'self-consciousnesses'. Since there is no mysterious, logically prior social entity whose good can cancel out the harm done to individuals, the pain or frustration suffered by any given person weighs heavily in the calculation of utility. And so the utilitarian, while denying the metaphysical status of natural rights, could actually provide a utilitarian justification for always respecting the freedoms they protect. Merleau-Ponty seems to be right: disputes about the ontological status of individuals and wholes are not politically innocent.

Marx's conception of 'man' as a social being also has *epistemological* significance. And here, too, we find an interesting contrast between Marxism and utilitarianism. Benthamite man is deemed to have a fully developed nature apart from society; he is essentially self-directing and self-sufficient. As a unique centre of consciousness, with distinctive thoughts and experiences, the individual alone knows who he is and what he desires. Because the individual is regarded as the best judge of his own interest (always assuming of course that his judgements are based on accurate and sufficient information) the public good, the 'greatest happiness of the greatest number', is merely an aggregation of the actual or expressed preferences of all the individuals in the society.

Marxists, on the other hand, view individual identity as socially derived. Our purposes, our knowledge, our aspirations —these are all *social* products. This rigorous environmental

[53] *Humanism and Terror*, 108.

determinism makes it plausible for Marxists to dismiss the empirical wishes of the working class. If individual consciousness is wholly shaped by external factors, then there is no reason to assume that a person's preferences are 'his own', self-directed rather than imposed or induced. When confronted by popular indifference or hostility, the Marxist need only identify the forces and agencies that have distorted the wants and values of the gullible masses. The groundwork is thus laid for the notorious Marxist distinction between the actual consciousness of the proletariat, and its 'true' or (in Lukács' idiom) 'imputed' consciousness.[54] One discovers the latter not through counting heads, but through scientific investigation and philosophical insight. Marx himself implied as much in a number of published and public statements. Consider the following example:

It is not a question of what this or that proletarian or even the whole proletariat momentarily *imagines* to be the aim. It is a question of *what* the proletariat *is* and what it *consequently* is historically compelled to do.[55]

In the *Communist Manifesto* he refers to communists as 'the most advanced and resolute section of the working class', who have 'the advantage of clearly understanding the line of march, the conditions, and the ultimate general results of the proletarian movement'.[56] The suggestion here is that the privileged few, gifted as they are with theoretical knowledge and speculative power, can take decisions for and act on behalf of the working class. And why should this vanguard, the repository of historical 'truth', wish to tolerate opposition —which, by definition, is spreading falsehood? Doesn't unqualified truth license unqualified authority? After all, majority consent adds nothing to the validity of a proposition which has been shown to be true, its validity being independent of how many people happen to grasp it. Marx and his followers believed, like Plato, that while error is multiple, truth is one. But if this is so there would appear to be nothing valuable

[54] G. Lukács, *History and Class Consciousness*, trans. R. Livingstone (Cambridge, Mass.: MIT Press, 1971), 51.
[55] *The Holy Family*, in *Writings of the Young Marx*, 368.
[56] *Marx & Engels: Basic Writings*, 20.

about diversity of opinion or majority rule. Monism and democratic decision-making would seem to be at odds, if not literally incompatible.

At this point I should anticipate a possible objection. What about the whole tradition of liberal rationalism, with its belief in apodictic moral laws? Didn't Locke, for example, advocate a kind of monism? Did he not believe in final truths about how human beings should behave? In reply, a number of points can be made. First, the liberal rationalists were indeed ambivalent about popular rule—in practice if not always in theory. They were 'fervent liberals but no more than timid democrats'.[57] Secondly, their assumption that man is pre-eminently a self-motivating, self-sufficient individual, endowed with natural rights, carries with it certain pertinent consequences. To begin with, it seems to rule out the idea of an élite vanguard whose task is to guide the masses down the path of salvation. On Locke's conception, for instance, the laws of nature require no esoteric or dialectical analysis; they are, as he phrased it, 'writ in the hearts of all Mankind', 'intelligible and plain to a rational creature'.[58] Moreover, the belief in individual rights poses strict limitations on what can be done in pursuit of truth. Hence Locke's famous observation that 'fire and sword' are not 'proper instruments wherewith to convince men's minds of error, and inform them of the truth'.[59] A liberal who is convinced of the rightness of his own ideas will nevertheless believe that some decisions *ought* to be left to the judgement of individuals, no matter how flawed, simply because, as distinct individuals, they alone have the right or (as utilitarians would prefer) the *detailed self-knowledge* to make them. Marxists, having discarded the concept of rights, together with its individualistic underpinnings, would seem to have no grounds for tolerating 'incorrect' behaviour or opinions.

[57] C. E. Lindblom, *Politics and Markets* (New York: Basic Books, 1977), 163.

[58] J. Locke, *Two Treatises of Government* (New York: Mentor, 1965); citations from *Second Treatise*, p. 315.

[59] J. Locke, *A Letter Concerning Toleration* (Indianapolis: Bobbs-Merrill, 1955), 26.

In any case, it would be misleading to conflate liberal dogmatism (if that is the appropriate word) with Marxist dogmatism. Liberals, however self-righteous, by and large accept
the imperfections of their fellow human beings and devise
social proposals or schemes that are attuned to these limitations. But Marxism, as we have seen, has a messianic component, which seeks to mould man after an abstract and
perfect pattern. There is a hidden link between Marx's epistemological holism and his assumption of (to use Talmon's
words) 'a preordained, harmonious and perfect scheme of
things, to which men are irresistibly driven'. Such an attitude
is obviously incompatible with utilitarianism, which sees the
actual social understandings of individual human beings as
the sole constituents of human reality. If society is simply the
pragmatic interaction of individual lives and perceptions, there
is no possibility of an overarching truth about the purpose of
society or existence. For the Marxist, however, reality cannot
be reduced to individual perceptions of it. Whether individuals
realize it or not, their lives are merely the medium of great
social forces. The way is thus open for politics to be converted
into the pursuit of absolute collective purposes, ordained by
history and wholly unrelated to the meagre aspirations of
ordinary, benighted people, incapable (as Lukács would say) of
grasping the 'totality'. And, as Talmon reminds us, a messianic
dictatorship is far worse than traditional forms of authoritarianism, for it displays contempt for social and cultural diversity. The desire to achieve 'abstract Man on a single level of
existence' (Talmon's phrasing) largely accounts for the most
striking feature of Marxism in practice: its totalitarian ambition to harness all social energies in the pursuit of common
goals. This ambition was implicit in Marx's demand to destroy
the barriers between state and civil society, to eliminate the
distinction between 'public' and 'private'. While this totalitarian urge need not lead to despotism or police terror, it is
bound to require a certain regimentation. This point was well
expressed by Nikita Khrushchev, the former Soviet leader
renowned for his detailed criticism of Stalin's crimes. To
those who clamoured for a more pluralistic approach to socialism, he offered the following words of Marxist folk wisdom:

As an orchestra conductor sees to it that all the instruments sound harmonious and in proportion, so in social and political life does the party direct the efforts of all people toward the achievement of a single goal. Each person must, like a bee in the hive, make his own contribution to increasing the material and spiritual wealth of society.[60]

This compulsive dream of beehive order projected upon an entire society, this passion for perfect co-ordination and integration, reflects the messianic longing for a final, global resolution of all contradictions and conflicts. And such a unitary vision is available only to those who go beyond the everyday perceptions of ordinary individuals and apprehend the grand social forces that will eventually solve the 'riddle of history'.

Consideration of this search for total harmony brings us to my third and final category: the ethical. Marx's reduction of 'the essence of man' to 'the ensemble of social relationships' implies a moral injunction to identify one's self-interest with communal well-being. Morality cannot be divorced from ontology. The pursuit of private interest can be plausibly justified only if we see human beings as essentially separate, rival centres of consciousness. To say this is not necessarily to deny the reality of social conditioning; it is simply to assert that something crucial remains when we abstract from an individual all those features which result from his social context. But if, as a matter of fact, 'the individual and generic life of man are not *distinct*',[61] if they are not opposed dimensions of being, then the natural expression of this radically socialized self would seem to be pursuit of the common interest. Marx certainly thought so. As has been shown, he condemned the fragmentation of the social body into isolated individuals, driven by egoism, who make a virtue out of selfishness and call it 'privacy'. He struck squarely at the nineteenth-century liberal elevation of the private conscience and the private realm of life. The public/private separation is, for Marx, no virtue but a vice that disappears in the course of social emancipation, when relations of co-operation and fraternity replace

---

[60] Reported in *Pravda*, 10 March 1963; translation from *Current Digest of the Soviet Press*, 15: 11 (23 Apr. 1963).

[61] *Economic and Philosophic Manuscripts* (1844), in *Writings of the Young Marx*, 306.

the competitive, 'inhuman' relationships fostered by capitalism. What Marx wanted was a true community in which the organic solidarity of agrarian life would be re-established in freer, more rational, and more splendid form. The cleavage between the particular and the common interest would disappear, as would the division of the human being into a 'public man' and a 'private man'. Co-operation would stem from a consciousness of common identity and shared interest, and express the deeply felt primacy and cohesion of the collective. This ideal society, communism, he defined in rhapsodic tones:

It is the *genuine* resolution of the antagonism between man and nature and between man and man; it is the true resolution of the conflict between existence and essence, objectification and self-affirmation, freedom and necessity, individual and species. It is the riddle of history solved.[62]

Here is the Kingdom of God without God: communism revives the Christian ideal of universal peace and absolute justice. This, however, is to be achieved not in some imaginary heaven, suspended above the natural order, but on earth itself, inhabited by real, flesh-and-blood creatures.

Intriguingly, Marx discovers his model of the communist future in the loving relationship between the sexes, where one can look beyond one's own needs and find fulfilment in the transcendence of self:

the relationship of man to woman is the *most natural* relationship of human being to human being. It thus indicates the extent to which man's *natural* behaviour has become *human* or the extent to which his *human* essence has become a *natural* essence for him, the extent to which his *human nature* has become *nature* to him. In this relationship is also apparent the extent to which man's *need* has become *human*, thus the extent to which the *other* human being, as human being, has become a need for him, the extent to which he in his most individual existence is at the same time a social being.[63]

While Marx's language may be obscure, his general point is clear: man becomes human (in the normative sense) only

---

[62] Ibid. 304.
[63] Ibid. 303.

when the needs of other human beings 'become a need for him'. The basic structural principle of loving sexual relations —mutual dependence and spontaneous reciprocity—must become a universal principle of social organization. In the same way that loving couples see themselves as an organic unit, the individual 'I' must be absorbed in the communist 'We'. 'Mine' and 'Thine' thus lose all meaning. It is necessary to be precise about the radical nature of Marx's message. He is not saying that the individual must *sacrifice* his or her private interests in the name of the common good. To Marx, the language of sacrifice is the language of bourgeois individualism. One must not, in the manner of Proudhon, juxtapose personal good and common good as though they were mutually exclusive entities, where the pursuit of one could only be at the expense of the other. The antithesis between public duty and private interest, or society and individual, exists only in bourgeois society and bourgeois minds.[64] As Marx wrote, 'The individual *is* the *social being.*' This is an ontological fact, which will rise to mass consciousness in the communist future, thus transforming human relationships. Where 'Need or satisfaction have ... lost their egoistic nature', where 'activity in direct association with others' becomes one's 'life expression', where the individual 'himself becomes social', one can no longer posit an imaginary contrast between 'individual' and 'collective'.[65] Communism is a world where individuals melt into one immense body—individuality transcends separateness, it abandons narcissism, to plunge into indivisible, communal substance.

It might be contended that this thickly-textured communitarianism was characteristic only of the early Marx, whose social criticism was still moralistic rather than scientific. According to this argument, the 'later' Marx, along with his disciples, saw communism as an objective historical necessity, springing from the dynamics of capitalism and the needs of the productive process; communism would not, and could not, come about through moral exhortation, through appeals to 'love', or 'togetherness', or 'communal feeling'. Indeed, such

---

[64] *The German Ideology,* in *Collected Works of Marx and Engels,* v, 213.

[65] *Economic and Philosophic Manuscripts* (1844), in *Writings of the Young Marx,* 306, 308.

sentiments would be irrelevant, for communism would be a realm of abundance where the satisfaction of one's needs would not depend upon the altruism of others.

This hypothetical objection to my exposition would be misleading, and for two reasons. First, the older Marx, while adopting a more detached, 'scientific' perspective, never abandoned his moral revulsion at the 'mutual indifference' of capitalist exchange relationships. In the *Grundrisse*, a work completed in 1858, he condemned the way in which capitalism forces us to view other people as instruments for the satisfaction of our own selfish interests. Though we may recognize our functional dependence upon each other, our behaviour is not motivated by the common interest. Marx thus calls for a world where 'sociality' governs social relationships, and where production is 'determined by communal needs and communal purposes'.[66]

The second reason why we must reject the hypothetical objection is this: if we reflect upon the slogan endorsed by all Marxists, 'From each according to his ability, to each according to his needs', we realize that it embodies a communitarianism of the most extreme sort. In a society observing this principle, the goods produced would in effect be collective goods, since all citizens would have a claim to enjoy them, irrespective of their personal contribution. Such a society would obviously fall apart unless individuals were prepared to work not for their own good alone but for the good of others. And such selflessness could only be sustained if individuals internalized the belief that their own good was inextricably intertwined with the good of others. The type of society envisaged by Marx and the Marxist tradition would depend, logically and practically, on a pervasive sense of communal solidarity. Even Lenin, the least sentimental of Marxists, laid stress on the necessity of communitarian attitudes. Speaking of communism, he observed:

'The narrow horizon of bourgeois law', which compels one to calculate with the heartlessness of a Shylock whether one has not worked half an hour more than somebody else, whether one is not getting less pay than somebody else—this narrow horizon will then be left

[66] *Grundrisse*, 244, 171.

behind. There will then be no need for society, in distributing products, to regulate the quantity to be received by each; each will take freely 'according to his needs'.[67]

Avarice, calculation, 'heartlessness'—these would disappear in what Gramsci described as a 'morally unitary social organism'.[68]

The despotic potential of Marxism's dream of 'oneness', a world without division, should be obvious. The attempt to do away with the sphere of privacy as an ultimate sanctuary holds out the prospect of a frightening politicization of the human psyche. Unrelenting communal solidarity requires loyalty, commitment, and obedience—all ideas that demand a sacrifice of individuality and private judgement. And what if the 'new socialist man' refuses to emerge? The materialistic theory of consciousness obliges Marxists to conceive human behaviour as malleable, a dependent variable. They consistently attribute our uncommunal attitudes and actions to the socializing effects of corrupt institutions, not to any permanent traits of human nature. But the question inevitably arises: who, if not human beings, actually created these debased institutions in the first place? If Hume was more right than wrong when he said that we, as a species, are characterized by 'Selfishness and Confin'd generosity', then Marxists are trying to foist an artificial unity on a reluctant humanity, to fit human beings into procrustean beds.[69] But even the most generous and unselfish of people might not wish to submerge their personal independence and private conscience for the sake of abstract ideals like 'community'. Full identification with the collectivity seems to clash with the prevailing concept of selfhood, which encourages individuals to look within themselves for the values that govern their lives. It is possible to dismiss this concept as a transient product of capitalism, but it is more plausible to view it as an inevitable consequence of modern life, as closed communities disintegrate under the impact of technology and industry, and

---

[67] V. I. Lenin, *The State and Revolution* (Moscow: Progress Publishers, 1949), 88.

[68] *Selections from the Prison Notebooks*, 259.

[69] D. Hume, *A Treatise of Human Nature*, ed. L. A. Selby-Bigge (Oxford: Clarendon Press, 1951), 495 (first pub. 1739).

social and geographic mobility. The fragmentation of the old order seriously weakens our ability to relate to others as members of a common moral or political world. And as the potential for collective solidarity (as envisaged by Marx) diminishes, exclusive forms of identification become more salient, at the same time multiplying the choices available to the individual. A modern person's self-definition will likely be influenced by a bewildering variety of factors: family, religion, wealth, nationality, occupation, gender, ethnicity. Marxism posits a fictitious harmony between the individual and the universal by prescinding from actual cultural identities. It is hard to imagine how the abolition of classes (in Marx's sense) could magically produce a world without fundamental conflicts of interest.

But even if Marx is right, even if we *are* essentially or potentially communal animals, capable of transcending our particularistic attachments, we would still disagree, and disagree violently, over what the common good is, and over how it is to be achieved. In a complex and multifaceted society, how can anything resembling unanimity be attained? The myriad claims on the public purse can be balanced in an infinite number of ways, depending upon individual tastes and judgements. Is the abundant flow of wealth preferable to the maintenance of traditional communities? Do new hospitals take priority over investment in energy resources? The list of difficult, emotionally charged alternatives is endless. Of course, if, like Marx, we presuppose the supersession of scarcity, the problem evaporates, since unlimited abundance obviates the need to face mutually exclusive choices. Marx genuinely believed that the technical progress already made under capitalism had fundamentally solved the problem of production, but that the shackles imposed on the productive forces by the capitalist system prevented this from being realized in practice. Unfortunately, the assumption of general plenitude, even within a single nation, is far-fetched. When we survey the world scene, as all socialists must, it appears ludicrous. In any case, the very idea of unlimited abundance stands in contradiction to Marx's conviction that human needs develop progressively through activity in transforming the world, for this conviction entails the proposition that needs are in principle limitless. It is therefore impossible to postulate an end-state where all needs are satisfied.

Marxism, then, suffers from an unrealizable aspiration to unity and wholeness. When Marxists gain power pressure naturally arises to move towards this illusory condition, to suppress discordant voices and activities, which, according to the canons of historical materialism, must express atavistic bourgeois interests. Kolakowski rightly concludes: 'The dream of perfect unity may come true only in the form of a carica-ture...as an artificial unity imposed by coercion from above.'[70] It might be argued, however, that if perfect unity fails to arise spontaneously, no genuine Marxist would seek to impose it—for Marxism, correctly construed, is all about the *self*-emancipation of the workers. Maybe so. But nagging doubts remain. Compare Marx's view of freedom with that of the liberals, and especially the utilitarians, who were by and large content to let individuals follow their own inner lights, choose their own plans of life or conceptions of the good. Conflict—of goals and interests—was accepted and even wel-comed as the unavoidable result of freedom. Marx, with his notion of false consciousness, had a rather different perspec-tive. For him a free society could not accommodate all the ends we might wish to pursue. Recall his words about human liberation being impossible if confined to man 'just as he is, corrupted by the entire organisation of our society, lost and alienated from himself'. Assessing the achievements of the French Revolution, Marx issued the following complaint: '...man was not freed from religion; he received religious freedom. He was not freed from property. He received free-dom of property. He was not freed from the egoism of trade but received freedom to trade.'[71] The implications are obvious: we do not liberate people by allowing them to speak freely, to form associations or worship as they please, or to dispose of their labour and property as they will. These are bogus free-doms, for they would still leave people in thrall to religion, property, and greed. Religious believers, defenders of private acquisition—all those who refuse to join the communist con-

[70] 'The Myth of Human Self-identity', 34.
[71] 'On the Jewish Question', in *Writings of the Young Marx*, 231, 240.

sensus are, in Marx's words, 'corrupted', 'lost and alienated'. Should we not prevent such people, mired as they are in indolence and superstition, from persisting in their harmful illusions? Should not such misguided folk consider themselves lucky if they are (in Rousseau's immortal phrase) 'forced to be free'? Upon taking power, Marxist revolutionists never agonize over the answer. Small wonder. The Marxist ideologue inhabits a simple and comforting world of certainties. He who is convinced that he has obtained the revelation of absolute truth, which has permitted him to understand once and for all the hidden nature of history, along with the secrets of human emancipation—such a person will find it easy to justify repression and cruelty if this, and this alone, is the price for the ultimate salvation of all men. Here I would expect a Marxist to cite the case of Rosa Luxemburg, an implacable and eminent radical, and an apparent exception to the 'rule' I am proposing. True, in attacking the Bolshevik handling of the 1917 Revolution, she advocated free elections, freedom of the press, and the rights of association and assembly;[72] yet she also urged the Russian leaders to crush all nationalist movements, purveyors of 'hollow, petty-bourgeois phraseology and humbug', with an iron hand, not suspecting for a moment that there might be any inconsistency between the two demands.[73] Luxemburg furnishes the exception that proves the rule. It is notable that she did not uphold political rights by appealing to 'some sort of abstract scheme of "justice"' or 'in terms of any other bourgeois-democratic phrases', but by reference to the particular 'social and economic relationships' for which they are designed. Individual freedom is to be valued only as a means to an end: the maintenance of revolutionary idealism and the construction of the socialist future. The Lenin–Trotsky approach was not immoral but futile and self-defeating.[74] However, where repression could actually serve the interests of the revolution (as in the case of the petty-bourgeois nationalists), there was no reason to shy away from it.

[72] R. Luxemburg, *The Russian Revolution* (London: Carl Slienger, 1977), 33–43.
[73] Ibid. 25.
[74] Ibid. 38, 39, 44–8.

*   *   *

There are some who will still try to deny the 'genetic link' between Marxism and the despotic regimes that have claimed to embody it. Such apologists doggedly seek to dissociate the innocent theory from the abominable practice. But what began as a laudable attempt to rescue Marx from his ignorant detractors (and supporters) has, I think, become a form of escapism. For Marxism, as a theory, suffers from an unresolved tension. On the one hand, it wishes to liberate man, to make him master of his own destiny; on the other, it seeks to confine him within a particular concept of the good life, to fit the diversity of human ends into a single pattern. Marxism's undoubted emancipatory ambitions are constantly subverted by its aspiration to 'wholeness', to a world without doubt, or contradiction, or conflict. What I have particularly tried to show is that this aspiration has its philosophical roots in Marx's belief that human beings are entirely constituted by their social relationships—which belief rendered him and his successors incapable of recognizing the distinctiveness and independence of the individual person.

Bibliography

ADLER, M., 'The Relation of Marxism to Classical German Philosophy', in *Austro-Marxism*, trans. and ed. T. Bottomore and P. Goode (Oxford: Clarendon Press, 1978), 62–8.

ALTHUSSER, L., *For Marx*, trans. B. Brewster (New York: Vintage Books, 1970).

ALTVATER, E., 'Notes on Some Problems of State Intervention', *Kapitalistate*, 1 (1973), 96–108.

AVINERI, S., *The Social and Political Thought of Karl Marx* (Cambridge: Cambridge University Press, 1968).

BAKUNIN, M., *Marxism, Freedom and the State*, trans. and ed. K. J. Kenafick (London: Freedom Press, 1984).

BAUER, O., 'Marxism and Ethics', in *Austro-Marxism*, trans. and ed. T. Bottomore and P. Goode (Oxford: Clarendon Press, 1978), 78–84.

BENTHAM, J., 'Anarchical Fallacies', in *Nonsense Upon Stilts: Bentham, Burke and Marx on the Rights of Man*, ed. J. Waldron (London: Methuen, 1987), 46–76.

BERLIN, I., 'Two Concepts of Liberty', in *Four Essays on Liberty* (Oxford: Oxford University Press, 1969).

—— *The Crooked Timber of Humanity: Chapters in the History of Ideas*, ed. H. Hardy (London: John Murray, 1990).

BERLINGUER, E., *La proposta comunista* (Turin: Einaudi, 1975).

BLOCH, E., 'Man and Citizen According to Marx', in *Socialist Humanism*, ed. E. Fromm (New York: Doubleday, 1966), 220–7.

BOBBIO, N., 'Is there a Marxist Theory of the State?', *Telos*, 35 (Spring 1978), 5–30.

—— *Which Socialism?*, ed. R. Bellamy and trans. R. Griffin (Cambridge: Polity Press, 1988).

BOGGS, C., 'The Democratic Road: New Departures and Old Problems', in *The Politics of Eurocommunism*, ed. C. Boggs and D. Plotke (London: Macmillan, 1980), 431–76.

BUCHANAN, A., *Marx and Justice: The Radical Critique of Liberalism* (London: Methuen, 1982).

CARRILLO, S., *Eurocommunism and the State* (Westport, Conn.: Lawrence Hill, 1978).

CLIFF, T., *Lenin*, vol. i, *Building the Party* (London: Pluto Press, 1975).

CLIFF, T., *Constitution (Fundamental Law) of the Union of Soviet Socialist Republics* (Moscow: Novosti Press Agency Publishing House, 1977).

CROCE, B., *Cultura e vita morale* (Bari: Laterza, 1955).

—— *Storia della storiografia italiana nel secolo decimonono*, ii (Bari: Laterza, 1964).

DELLA VOLPE, G., *Rousseau e Marx* (Rome: Riuniti, 1957).

—— 'The Legal Philosophy of Socialism', in *Socialist Humanism*, ed. E. Fromm (New York: Doubleday, 1966), 425–40.

DRAGSTEDT, A., and SLAUGHTER, C., *State, Power and Bureaucracy* (London: New Park Publications, 1981).

DWORKIN, R., *Taking Rights Seriously* (London: Duckworth, 1977).

EASTON, D., *The Political System* (New York: Alfred A. Knopf, 1953).

ELLEINSTEIN, J., 'The Skein of History Unrolled Backwards', in *Eurocommunism*, ed. G. R. Urban (London: Maurice Temple Smith, 1978), 73–96.

ELSTER, J., *Making Sense of Marx* (Cambridge: Cambridge University Press, 1985).

FEHER, F., 'The Dictatorship over Needs', *Telos*, 35 (Spring 1978), 31–42.

FEMIA, J. V., 'Elites, Participation and the Democratic Creed', *Political Studies*, 27 (Mar. 1979), 1–20.

—— *Gramsci's Political Thought* (Oxford: Clarendon Press, 1981).

GERAS, N., *Marx and Human Nature: Refutation of a Legend* (London: Verso, 1983).

GERTH, H. H., and MILLS, C. W. (eds.), *From Max Weber: Essays in Sociology* (London: Routledge and Kegan Paul, 1970).

GRAHAM, K., *The Battle of Democracy: Conflict, Consensus and the Individual* (Brighton: Wheatsheaf Books, 1986).

GRAMSCI, A., *L'Ordine Nuovo: 1919–1920* (Turin: Einaudi, 1954).

—— *Scritti giovanili: 1914–1918* (Turin: Einaudi, 1958).

—— *Selections from the Prison Notebooks*, ed. and trans Q. Hoare and G. Nowell Smith (London: Lawrence and Wishart, 1971).

—— *Selections from Political Writings: 1910–1920*, ed. Q. Hoare and trans. J. Mathews (London: Lawrence and Wishart, 1977).

GRIPP, R. C., *The Political System of Communism* (London: Nelson, 1973).

HAHN, W. G., 'Electoral "Choice" in the Soviet Bloc', *Problems of Communism*, 36 (March/Apr. 1987), 29–39.

HANDS, G., 'Roberto Michels and the Study of Political Parties', *British Journal of Political Science*, 1 (Apr. 1971), 155–72.

HAYEK, F. A., *The Road to Serfdom* (London: Routledge and Kegan Paul, 1976).

HEGEL, G. W. F., *Philosophy of Right*, trans. and ed. T. M. Knox (Oxford: Clarendon Press, 1952).

HOFFMAN, J., *Marxism and the Theory of Praxis* (London: Lawrence and Wishart, 1975).

HOUGH, J. F., 'Political Participation in the Soviet Union', *Soviet Studies*, 28 (Jan. 1976), 3–20.

HUME, D., *A Treatise of Human Nature*, ed. L. A. Selby-Bigge (Oxford: Clarendon Press, 1951).

HUNT, R. N., *The Political Ideas of Marx and Engels*, i (London: Macmillan, 1975).

JESSOP, B., *The Capitalist State* (Oxford: Martin Robertson, 1982).

JOHNSTON, L., *Marxism, Class Analysis and Socialist Pluralism* (London: Allen & Unwin, 1986).

KASE, F. J., *People's Democracy* (Leiden: A. W. Sijthoff, 1968).

KAUTSKY, J., *Communism and the Politics of Development, Persistent Myths and Changing Behaviour* (New York: Wiley, 1968).

KAUTSKY, K., *La questione agraria* (Milan: Feltrinelli, 1959).

—— *The Class Struggle*, trans. W. E. Bohn (New York: W. W. Norton, 1971).

—— *Selected Political Writings*, ed. and trans. P. Goode (London: Macmillan, 1983).

—— *The Materialist Conception of History*, trans. R. Meyer and J. H. Kautsky (New Haven, Conn.: Yale University Press, 1988).

KISS, A., *Marxism and Democracy* (Budapest: Akadémiai Kiado, 1982).

KOESTLER, A., *Darkness at Noon* (Harmondsworth, Middx.: Penguin, 1964).

KOLAKOWSKI, L., 'The Myth of Human Self-identity', in *The Socialist Idea*, ed. L. Kolakowski and S. Hampshire (London: Weidenfeld and Nicolson, 1974), 18–35.

—— 'Marxist Roots of Stalinism', in *Stalinism*, ed. R. C. Tucker (New York: W. W. Norton, 1977), 283–98.

—— *Main Currents of Marxism*, vol. i, *The Founders* (Oxford: Oxford University Press, 1981).

KORSCH, K., *Three Essays on Marxism* (London: Pluto Press, 1971).

—— *Revolutionary Theory*, ed. D. Kellner (Austin: University of Texas Press, 1977).

KOSIK, K., 'The Individual and History', in *Marx and the Western World*, ed. N. Lobkowicz (Notre Dame: University of Notre Dame Press, 1967), 177–91.

LAMPERT, N., 'The Dilemmas of *Glasnost*', *The Journal of Communist Studies*, 4 (Dec. 1988), 48–63.

LENIN, V. I., *The Proletarian Revolution and the Renegade Kautsky* (London: Martin Lawrence, 1935).

LENIN, V. I., *The State and Revolution* (Moscow: Progress Publishers, 1949).

—— 'The Immediate Tasks of the Soviet Government', in *Collected Works*, xxvii (Moscow: Progress Publishers, 1960–70), 235–78.

—— 'Report on the Party Programme', in *Collected Works*, xxix (Moscow: Progress Publishers, 1960–70), 165–96.

—— 'On Trade Unions', in *Collected Works*, xxxii (Moscow: Progress Publishers, 1960–70), 19–42.

—— *What is to be Done?* (Moscow: Progress Publishers, 1967).

LEVIN, M., *Marx, Engels and Liberal Democracy* (London: Macmillan, 1989).

LICHTHEIM, G., *Marxism* (London: Routledge and Kegan Paul, 1961).

LINDBLOM, C., *Politics and Markets* (New York: Basic Books, 1977).

LIVELY, J., *Democracy* (Oxford: Basil Blackwell, 1975).

LOCKE, J., *A Letter Concerning Toleration* (Indianapolis: Bobbs-Merrill, 1955).

—— *Two Treatises of Government* (New York: Mentor, 1965).

LOMBARDO RADICE, L., 'Communism With an Italian Face', in *Eurocommunism*, ed. G. R. Urban (London: Maurice Temple Smith, 1978), 32–57.

LUKÁCS, G., *History and Class Consciousness*, trans. R. Livingstone (Cambridge, Mass.: MIT Press, 1971).

LUKES, S., *Marxism and Morality* (Oxford: Clarendon Press, 1985).

LUXEMBURG, R., *The Mass Strike, the Political Party and the Trade Unions*, first pub. 1906 (London: Merlin Press, n.d.).

—— *Reform or Revolution* (New York: Pathfinder Press, 1970).

—— *The Russian Revolution* (London: Carl Slienger, 1977).

MACKIE, J. L., 'Can There be a Right-based Moral Theory?', *Midwest Studies in Philosophy*, vol. iii, *Studies in Ethical Theory* (1978), 350–9.

MACPHERSON, C. B., *The Real World of Democracy* (New York: Oxford University Press, 1972).

MANDEL, E., *Marxist Economic Theory*, ii (New York: Monthly Review Press, 1968).

MANSBRIDGE, J., *Beyond Adversary Democracy* (Chicago: University of Chicago Press, 1983).

MARCUSE, H., 'Repressive Tolerance', in *A Critique of Pure Tolerance*, ed. R. P. Wolff *et al.* (Boston: Beacon Press, 1967), 90, 100–1.

—— *One-Dimensional Man* (London: Sphere Books, 1972).

MARKOVIĆ, M., 'Socialism and Self-management', *Praxis*, 1 (1965).

—— *The Contemporary Marx: Essays on Humanist Communism* (Nottingham: Spokesman Books, 1974).

—— 'Stalinism and Marxism', in *Stalinism*, ed. R. C. Tucker (New York: W. W. Norton, 1977), 299–318.

MARX, K., *Capital*, iii (Moscow: Foreign Languages Publishing House, 1959).

—— *Writings of the Young Marx on Philosophy and Society*, trans. and ed. L. D. Easton and K. H. Guddat (New York: Doubleday, 1967).

—— *The Civil War in France* (Peking: Foreign Languages Press, 1970).

—— *Grundrisse*, trans. M. Nicolaus (Harmondsworth, Middx.: Penguin, 1973).

—— *Capital*, i (Harmondsworth, Middx.: Penguin, 1976).

—— *Selected Writings*, ed. and trans. D. McLellan (Oxford: Oxford University Press, 1977).

MARX, K., and ENGELS, F., *Selected Correspondence: 1846–1895* (New York: International Publishers, 1942).

—— —— *Basic Writings on Politics and Philosophy*, ed. L. S. Feuer (New York: Doubleday, 1959).

—— —— *The German Ideology*, in *The Collected Works of Marx and Engels*, v (London: Lawrence and Wishart, 1975).

—— —— *Selected Works*, ii (Moscow: Progress Publishers, 1976).

MEDVEDEV, F., and KULIKOV, G., *Human Rights and Freedoms in the USSR*, trans. L. Lezhneva (Moscow: Progress Publishers, 1981).

MERLEAU-PONTY, M., *Humanism and Terror*, trans. J. O'Neill (Boston: Beacon Press, 1969).

MILL, J. S., 'On Liberty', in *Utilitarianism, Liberty, and Representative Government* (London: Dent, 1910).

MOORE, B., *Soviet Politics: The Dilemma of Power* (Cambridge, Mass.: Harvard University Press, 1950).

MOSCA, G., *The Ruling Class*, ed. A. Livingston and trans. H. D. Kahn (New York: McGraw-Hill, 1939).

NAPOLITANO, G., *The Italian Road to Socialism*, an interview with E. Hobsbawm (Westport: Lawrence Hill, 1977).

NELSON, R., 'Assessing Private Enterprise: An Exegesis of Tangled Doctrine', *The Bell Journal of Economics*, 12 (Spring 1981), 93–111.

NOVE, A., *The Economics of Feasible Socialism* (London: Allen & Unwin, 1983).

PAINE, T., *The Rights of Man* (Harmondsworth, Middx.: Penguin, 1969).

PASIĆ, N., 'The Idea of Direct Self-managing Democracy and

Socialization of Policy-making', in *Self-governing Socialism*, ed. B. Horvat, M. Marković, and R. Supek (White Plains: International Arts and Sciences Press, 1975), 34–40.

PLEKHANOV, G., *The Development of the Monist View of History* (Moscow: Progress Publishers, 1956).

POULANTZAS, N., 'The Problem of the Capitalist State', in *Ideology in Social Science*, ed. R. Blackburn (London: Fontana, 1972), 238–53.

—— *Political Power and Social Classes* (London: New Left Books, 1973).

—— 'The Capitalist State: A Reply to Miliband and Laclau', *New Left Review*, 95 (1976), 63–83.

RIGBY, T. H., 'Hough on Political Participation in the Soviet Union', *Soviet Studies*, 28 (Apr. 1976), 257–61.

ROUSSEAU, J.-J., *The Social Contract and Discourses*, trans. and ed. G. D. H. Cole (London: Dent, 1913).

RUSSELL, B., *What is Democracy?* (London: Allen & Unwin, 1946).

SALVADORI, M., *Karl Kautsky and the Socialist Revolution: 1880–1938*, trans. J. Rothschild (London: New Left Books, 1979).

SARTORI, G., *Democratic Theory* (Detroit: Wayne State University Press, 1962).

SCHAPIRO, L., *The Government and Politics of the Soviet Union* (London: Hutchinson, 1967).

SCHECTER, D., *Gramsci and the Theory of Industrial Democracy* (Aldershot: Gower, 1991).

SCHUMPETER, J. A., *Capitalism, Socialism and Democracy*, 3rd edn. (New York: Harper & Row, 1950).

SELUCKY, R., *Marxism, Socialism, Freedom* (London: Macmillan, 1979).

SHUB, D., *Lenin* (Harmondsworth, Middx.: Penguin, 1966).

SKILLING, H. G., '"People's Democracy" in Soviet Theory—II', *Soviet Studies*, 3: 2 (1951), 131–49.

SMITH, G. W., 'Marxian Metaphysics and Individual Freedom', in *Marx and Marxisms*, ed. G. H. R. Parkinson (Cambridge: Cambridge University Press, 1982), 229–42.

STALIN, J., *Problems of Leninism* (Moscow: Progress Publishers, 1945).

SUCHTING, W., 'Marx's Theses on Feuerbach', in *Issues in Marxist Philosophy*, ed. J. Mepham and D. H. Ruben, vol. ii (Brighton: Harvester, 1979), 5–34.

SUPEK, R., 'The Sociology of Workers' Self-management', in *Self-governing Socialism*, ed. B. Horvat, M. Marković, and R. Supek (White Plains: International Arts and Sciences Press, 1975), 3–13.

TALMON, J. L., *The Origins of Totalitarian Democracy* (Harmondsworth, Middx.: Penguin, 1987).

THUCYDIDES, *The Peloponnesian War*, trans. and ed. R. Warner (Baltimore: Penguin, 1954).

TOCQUEVILLE, A. DE, *Democracy in America*, ii, ed. P. Bradley (New York: Vintage Books, 1945).

TOGLIATTI, P., *On Gramsci and Other Writings*, ed. and trans. D. Sassoon (London: Lawrence and Wishart, 1979).

TROTSKY, L., 'Their Morals and Ours', in *Their Morals and Ours: Marxist versus Liberal Views on Morality*, four essays by L. Trotsky, J. Dewey, and G. Novack, 4th edn. (New York: Pathfinder Press, 1969).

TUCKER, D. F. B., *Marxism and Individualism* (Oxford: Basil Blackwell, 1980).

TUCKER, R. C. (ed.), *The Marx–Engels Reader* (New York: W. W. Norton, 1972).

—— *The Lenin Anthology* (New York: W. W. Norton, 1975).

ULC, O., 'Legislative Politics in Czechoslovakia', in *Communist Legislatures in Comparative Perspective*, ed. D. Nelson and S. White (Albany: SUNY Press, 1982), 111–24.

VAJDA, M., *The State and Socialism* (London: Allison and Busby, 1981).

VERNON, R., 'Moral Pluralism and the Liberal Mind', in *Unity, Plurality and Politics: Essays in Honour of F. M. Barnard*, ed. J. M. Porter and R. Vernon (London: Croom Helm, 1986), 143–61.

WALLER, M., *Democratic Centralism* (Manchester: Manchester University Press, 1981).

WHITE, S., 'Reforming the Electoral System', *The Journal of Communist Studies*, 4 (Dec. 1988), 1–17.

WIATR, J., and PRZEWORSKI, A., 'Control Without Opposition', *Government and Opposition*, 1 (1965–6), 227–39.

ZAKRZEWSKI, W., 'The Mechanism of Popular Activity in the Exercise of State Authority in People's Poland', in *Representation*, ed. J. R. Pennock and J. W. Chapman (New York: Atherton Press, 1968).

Index